American Polish Owczarek Nizinny Club

The Official Book of
The Polish Lowland Sheepdog

T.F.H. Publications, Inc., is pleased to collaborate with the American Polish Owczarek Nizinny Club (APONC) and its esteemed authors to produce this official breed book. The publisher wishes to acknowledge the dedicated efforts of Betty Augustowski, PON breeder and President of the American Rare Breed Association (ARBA), without whose cooperation this volume could not have been possible. It is hoped that *The Official Book of the Polish Lowland Sheepdog* brings the breed much deserved recognition and wins it new fanciers throughout the English-speaking world.

Marcy Myerovich
Editor

Distributed in the UNITED STATES to the Pet Trade by T.F.H. Publications, Inc., One T.F.H. Plaza, Neptune City, NJ 07753; distributed in the UNITED STATES to the Bookstore and Library Trade by National Book Network, Inc. 4720 Boston Way, Lanham MD 20706; in CANADA to the Pet Trade by H & L Pet Supplies Inc., 27 Kingston Crescent, Kitchener, Ontario N2B 2T6; Rolf C. Hagen Ltd., 3225 Sartelon Street, Montreal 382 Quebec; in CANADA to the Book Trade by Vanwell Publishing Ltd., 1 Northrup Crescent, St. Catharines, Ontario L2M 6P5 ; in ENGLAND by T.F.H. Publications, PO Box 15, Waterlooville PO7 6BQ; in AUSTRALIA AND THE SOUTH PACIFIC by T.F.H. (Australia), Pty. Ltd., Box 149, Brookvale 2100 N.S.W., Australia; in NEW ZEALAND by Brooklands Aquarium Ltd. 5 McGiven Drive, New Plymouth, RD1 New Zealand; in Japan by T.F.H. Publications, Japan—Jiro Tsuda, 10-12-3 Ohjidai, Sakura, Chiba 285, Japan; in SOUTH AFRICA by Lopis (Pty) Ltd., P.O. Box 39127, Booysens, 2016, Johannesburg, South Africa. Published by T.F.H. Publications, Inc.
MANUFACTURED IN THE UNITED STATES OF AMERICA
BY T.F.H. PUBLICATIONS, INC.

The Official Book of
The Polish Lowland Sheepdog

By
E. Jane Brown
Tomasz Borkowski, DVM, PhD
Margaret Supronowicz, DVM

E. Jane Brown

Dedication

In loving memory of Elizabeth Jane Arnold Brown.
(September 16, 1944—December 2, 1991)
Jane was in the midst of writing this book when the ravages of
diabetes overtook her. Our heartfelt thanks go to Jane for doing so much
to document and establish this breed in America.

Acknowledgments

Betty Augustowski—for coordinating information for the book after the death of Jane Brown.

Mary Von Drehle—for endless hours of work with additions and corrections.

Andrez Stepinski—for sending valuable information from Poland.

Dorene Zalis—for the chapter on grooming, taken from *The Herder*.

Contents

The Polski Owczarek Nizinny is a happy, spirited breed of dog that is winning new admirers with each passing day. Posing for the camera on the occasion of her first birthday is Shaggi Pons S Brandy, by Ch. Shaggi Pons Duzy Bozolski ex Ch. Kluska z Elzbieta. Breeders, Loana Shields and Tom Wason. Owner, Phyllis Vlasaty.

How Do You Say That?

The first step in getting to know the "shaggy dog with the unpronounceable name," as it is so often referred to, is learning to say Polski Owczarek Nizinny. Polski, obviously, translates to Polish and is pronounced *pol' skee*. Owczarek—sheepdog—is trickier; the w sounds like a v, and cz has a ch sound, *ahv cha' rek*. Nizinny, meaning lowland, is pronounced like this—*ni gi' nee*, with the soft g sounding like the g in mirage and collage.

The Polish Lowland Sheepdog is so named to differentiate it from the Owczarek Podhalanski (Polish Tatra dog), the sheepdog of the Podhale mountain region of southern Poland.

With the intriguing name of this intriguing breed mastered, you will want to know that in Poland and generally in the U.S., these dogs are referred to as PONs. In some continental European countries and in Britain, PONs have come to be known as Nizinnies. This caused some confusion in the early years in the U.S., but the American Polish Owczarek Nizinny Club (APONC), the official parent club in the U.S., prefers PON to Nizinny, because it is simpler and is what the breed is known as in its native land.

Keeping an eye on things is "Cas," formally known as SKC Ch. Europa Casimir z Elzbieta CD. The PON's ancestors were highly valued by shepherds and farmers.

Smok z Kordegardy, known as the father of the present-day PON. He was the foundation dog at Kordegardy Kennels, and his name appears in the pedigrees of many charnpion PONs.

A trio of famous PONs from Poland: Inkluz z Kordegardy, Isia z Kordegardy, and Hajda z Kordegardy.

History of the Breed

DOG MEETS MAN

Dogs are the only animals that man did not have to conquer to befriend or control. Dogs came willingly to the campfires of early man to share his food and protect their mutual interests. Bonds were struck in those prehistoric times that have survived and strengthened through the ages. Dogs have become invaluable to man as assistant and friend, and they have benefited from this liaison as no other species has in the animal kingdom. This bond became so beneficial and necessary to the dog that today he cannot exist without man. To more fully appreciate and understand that four-footed shaggy imp you've become interested in, it is helpful to at least browse through the annals of his family history.

TIBETAN ROOTS

The Polski Owczarek Nizinny is a very old breed of dog, but not an ancient breed. It is widely believed that the PON, and many other heavily coated purebred breeds that we see today, descended from dogs originally developed in Central Asia: the Tibetan Mastiff, the Tibetan Spaniel, the Lhasa Apso, and the Tibetan Terrier. It is not certain that all of these breeds had the same ancestor, but they are all shaggy and have long coats of different types and colors. The high mountains and huge valleys in Asia isolated people and undoubtedly challenged them to produce separate breeds for special purposes. It is known that Tibet had always engaged in foreign trade, so it is conceivable that, besides silk and gold, some of her native breeds were traded as well. That would explain the similarities in so many canine breeds that have originated from different parts of the world.

SHEEPDOGS ON THE MOVE

When nomadic tribes from the East migrated to Europe, dogs were already being used by man in war, in hunting, and in guarding and maneuvering herds of livestock. Westward routes probably took some migrants through mountain passes into southern Europe, while some pushed into Russia. Harry Glover, in his book *Purebred Dogs*, suggests that the Huns, who relied heavily on animal herding and the plundering of sedentary peoples, were instrumental in populating the Western World with a varied assortment of related sheepdogs. The large, heavily coated sheepdogs that accompanied the Huns on their rampages through Europe during

Smok z Kordegardy with his grandson Arak Greps. Smok was a dog that possessed excellent conformation and type, which Polish PON breeders strove to emulate in their own dogs. Photo by H. Skalska.

the latter part of the fourth century AD were probably interbred with local dogs to produce working dogs with specific traits and functions. As man crossed new frontiers, dog types evolved that were suited to the terrain, the climate, and the type of work required. New breeds became indigenous when characteristics became fixed by acclimation and by selective breeding.

GUARDS AND HERDERS

Historically, two kinds of shepherd dogs were known: flock guards and flock herders. Flock guardians were large and muscular and could fight the likes of bears, wolves and lynx, while also alerting the herdsmen. These Molosser-type dogs were usually white to blend in with the sheep and goats. They can be found, even today, all over Europe—the Pyrenees Mountain Dog, the Turkish Anatolian, the Italian Maremma, the Hungarian Komondor and Kuvasz, the Szarplaninac from Yugoslavia, and the Polish Tatra dog. The large dogs frightened the sheep and were too aggressive for gentle work, especially with lambs. The shepherd needed a handy, fast, intelligent dog to help with the care of the flock. For this purpose the smaller sheepdog was developed. This herding sheepdog guided the flock to the pasture, kept it together, and prevented the flock from venturing toward water or other obstacles. Young shepherd dogs lived with the sheep, played with the lambs, and grew up as part of the flock.

PONs belong to one of the most numerous families of herding dogs. They exhibit certain basic characteristics of the smaller sheepdog—a tendency for a squarely built body; a smooth, efficient trot; a strong, long protective coat; a loyal personality with strong herding instincts; a suspicion of strangers; a highly developed sense of territory; and a strong sense of independence. These dogs greatly helped people with herding work while leaving space for the larger dogs to protect the livestock from wild animals. Besides the Polski Owczarek Nizinny, there were similar dogs in the bordering countries of Russia, Germany, Czechoslovakia, and Hungary.

Maxwell Riddle, in his book

It is the dedicated efforts of Dr. Danuta Hryniewicz that have brought about the resurgence of the Polski Owczarek Nizinny. Today, the breed is enjoying rising popularity on both sides of the Atlantic. Photo by R. Rzepecki.

Dogs Through History, tells us that in ancient Greek, Egyptian, and Israeli literature, the shepherds and shepherd dogs were not generally held in high esteem. They were actually despised. Perhaps the streak of stubbornness that you can sometimes detect in your PON is a reflection of his inherent determination to survive.

LUCKY DOGS

The PON is indeed a survivor. The 20th-century PON brings with him a litany of hard-luck stories that span centuries. PONs are only one of hundreds of diverse types of hunting, herding, and guard dogs developed in the last two millenniums to assist man. Sadly, many of the old European working breeds have disappeared as a result of changes in the lifestyles and needs of modern man. The repercussions of two global wars have also rendered many breeds extinct or near extinction. Only the most useful, the fittest, and the luckiest survive. The PON's working ability, intense desire to please, and compatible nature have carried him through turbulent times.

EARLY PONS

Medium-sized, shaggy-coated herding dogs were known and selectively bred in Poland for centuries, mostly in eastern and northern districts. It is through direct records, ancient drawings, rock carvings, and old graves that we can trace the full development of the breed. The first written

Int., Pol., Czech. Ch. Doman z Kordegardy, by Lider z Kordegardy ex Certa z Kordegardy. This dog is also a two-time Certificate of Aptitude for Championship of International Beauty (CACIB) winner.

document about a medium-sized herding dog in Poland that worked with hundreds of sheep is from the 13th century. Herds of cultivated animals, often imported from abroad, were tended by shepherds with medium-sized hairy dogs. The next written information about Polish sheepdogs is from 1514. Mrs. Willson's book *The Bearded Collie* documents a written contract between Polish ship owner K. Grabski from Gdansk and a Scottish sheep breeder. Grabski sailed from Poland to trade grain for the hardiest Scottish sheep. He was accompanied by six sheepdogs, whose job it was to separate 20 sheep chosen by Grabski out of a flock of 60. The Scot was so impressed with the adept work of the dogs that he offered to exchange an additional pair of sheep for one male and two female sheepdogs. Mrs. Willson believes that shaggy dogs were introduced to the British Isles about 2,000 BC and that the Polski Owczarek Nizinny helped to develop the present type of Bearded Collie.

Christopher Kluk, from the parish of Ciechanowiec, Poland, wrote in his books on farming, hunting, and natural history, dated 1779, that he was familiar with very intelligent, hairy, shaggy white dogs, mostly without tails, that can be easily identified as PON-type. The term "poodle" (Hirtenpudel or Schaferpudel in Germany) was used to designate shaggy-coated dogs. According to Kluk, "Poodles usually medium (sized), shaggy, are the most

A postage stamp honoring the PON. It was issued in 1962.

clever dogs, having almost human intelligence. No other dog can be compared to them in herding flocks." In another book, he also wrote that they were selectively bred.

Another paper from somewhere between 1783 and 1785 was written by Princess Jablonowska of Podlasie in northeast Poland. She established rules to be followed on her farmland estates that every herd of 1,000 sheep should be watched by three people, two big dogs for protection, and two smaller dogs. She commented on the superb working qualities of the smaller dogs.

Also, a medium-sized type of herding dog was known in another region of Poland—near Lublin. From the 18th century, gentle, intelligent, hairy dogs were used on large farms to keep the herds of sheep together during the day and to act as watch dogs around the houses at night. They were selected not for conformation of good head, ears, or color, but

Dr. Hryniewicz and some of her Kordegardy dogs: Lemat, Domka, Hajda, Isia, Inkluz, Harfa, and Milek. Photo by J. Kopec.

for good quality of long protective hair that did not easily mat, good herding instinct, good temperament, and the ability to utilize food well.

This robust utility dog was perfectly suited to the harsh conditions of his natural habitat in Polish farmland. PONs worked outdoors in all weather conditions without the benefit of regular food. Only the hardiest and most intelligent specimens of man and animal survived in those days.

FIRST SHOW DOGS

At the end of the 19th century in Poland, farm animal shows became popular. It was customary to show herding dogs along with the farm animals. This time period was very difficult for Poland; the country was divided into three different parts. At the first such show in 1881, there was only one herding dog presented.

NO SHEEP TO HERD

By the beginning of the 20th century, sheep farming was not a thriving industry, and hairy herding dogs were less and less popular among farmers. Farmers who no longer had sheep did not care about sheepdogs. PONs were not called "purebreds" at the time, merely working dogs. There was no interest in pedigrees and conformation. Some old farmers still kept sheepdogs around, mainly out of sentiment.

PIONEER BREEDERS

After World War I, when Poland became independent after long years of occupation, there was an increased interest in purebred Polish animals. The first person to turn her attention to these clever little country dogs was Countess Maria J. Czetwertynska Grocholska, who lived in Planta near Radzyn in eastern Poland. She bought several dogs from old shepherds and began, possibly for the first time in the history of the breed, to selectively breed for type and appearance. In 1924, she exhibited the first two Polski Owczarek Nizinny at the Show of Poultry, Pigeons and Dogs in Warsaw. The dogs were without pedigree. Her kennel existed until 1941 and for many years she regularly showed dogs she had bred.

From Mrs. Grocholska's stock, Wanda and Roza Zoltowska from Milanow near Radzyn began breeding PONs in the 1930s. They bred five generations starting with Fajkus and Tuska. Wanda Zoltowska wrote that all of the dogs that they had bred, as well as other sheepdogs they had seen in their region, were similar in type, being medium sized, white, some with cream patches, and most with natural bobtails. They also observed that all the dogs were excellent herders of sheep and cattle, and also functioned as guards and intelligent, friendly pets. They were also used for tracking boars. Zoltowska Kennels existed for 12 years. Altogether, from these two kennels, 17 Polish Sheepdogs were exhibited at

Smok z Kordegardy. Smok, whose name in English translates into "dragon," was highly renowned for his herding abilities.

shows from 1924 through 1937. The active and successful breeding and showing activities of these three ladies significantly influenced the popularity of the breed.

PON REVIVAL

As national pride continued to escalate in Poland, dog enthusiasts tried to establish and register purebred Polish breeds. In 1937 the Working Dogs Society put a notice in their official paper, "My Dog," about a research program on the Polish Sheepdog. They solicited information on dogs living in the country with farmers, regardless of known pedigrees. All

Three–month–old Rzepicha z Psiego Raju, by Doman z Kordegardy ex Szelma z Kordegardy, and five–month–old Zyndram z Kordegardy, by Lubek z Kordegardy ex Hajda z Kordegardy.

Int., Pol., Czech. Ch. Doman z Kordegardy pictured during a break at a dog show in Poland. The PON has contributed to the development of several other herding breeds, including the Bearded Collie.

owners of Polish sheepdogs or anyone knowing of this type of dog were asked to send in as much information as they could about the breed, such as: where a number of the dogs could be located; how long the dogs had existed in that region; the names of long-time breeders of Polish sheepdogs; and an exact description of the dogs they had encountered or owned. A photo of Wanda Zoltowska's foundation bitch, Tuska z Planty, was printed with the notice. The resurgence of the breed was imminent.

WAR BREAKS OUT

Unfortunately, all the work done on behalf of the breed was in vain. When World War II broke out, all dog activities in Poland were halted, dogs were lost, documents were destroyed, and the Polish people focused their attention on survival. Wanda Zoltowska, in her paper *Owczarki Nizinne z Milanowa*, recounts a tale of her bitch Psyche. Psyche stayed with Wanda during the bombardment of Warsaw in 1944. She was always first to alert people and urge them to go to the underground shelter before the explosions began. Thanks to her, many people survived this terrible time in underground shelters while their apartment buildings above were demolished. This capability to warn people of impending peril also allowed Psyche to survive a time when the starving people of Warsaw were happy to find a dog or cat. By serving people in a very important way, Psyche was able to survive

Dr. Hryniewicz and Doman. Many of Dr. Hryniewicz's dogs attained championship status, and they passed their excellent qualities on to their offspring.

the war. Ms. Zoltowska did survive the war with two of her dogs. She and her dogs resettled in Krakow, but details of her continued interest in dogs are unknown.

MORE PIONEERS

After the war, dog activists formed the Polish Kennel Club in 1948. The Bydgoszcz Branch of the Polish Kennel Club and Maria Dubrowinowa attempted to rescue and reestablish the breed soon after the war ended. They resumed the investigation of

Polish sheepdogs among farmers in the northern region of Poland. They selected quality dogs for pre-registration, which meant any dog that resembled a PON was registered, given a number, and could be used in a breeding program. Only good-quality puppies could then be used for second generation breeding. When a dog had three generations of known ancestors, he could be registered and receive an official pedigree. The first kennel to register PONs, in 1957, belonged to Mrs. Kusinowicz of Babia Wies Kennels. She had been breeding PONs since 1946.

Dr. Hryniewicz with Domka z Kordegardy (the lighter-colored dog), a CWC winner. Photo by Jan Kopec.

PILLAR OF THE BREED

The person who has done the most in terms of breeding and promoting the modern-day PON is decidedly Dr. Danuta Hryniewicz. She is a veterinarian who began her practice around Poland's seashore district after World War II. On her rounds she encountered an old farmer who owned two sheepdogs, the kind Dr. Hryniewicz had seen frequently in prewar days around Poznan and Lwow. She remembered them as being highly valued by shepherds. She asked the farmer to save her one of the offspring from a future litter by his dogs, Kurta and Laska; she was involved in breeding other breeds at that time. It was not until several years later that Dr. Hryniewicz was given the bitch Laska in whelp. The dog was quite old by now and delivered only one puppy. Using her established kennel name, she named the pup Smok z Kordegardy. "Smok" means "dragon."

Since she had no plans for breeding this new breed at that time, the dog was given to a local shepherd and became well known by other farmers for his excellent herding ability. Several years later, Dr. Hryniewicz came across an article in a dog publication about a herding breed native to Poland that was well known in prewar days. From the picture that accompanied the article and the description, she realized that it fit the description of her Smok. She contacted her local kennel club, which put her in contact with Mrs. Kusinowicz's Babia

Polish dog breeds gathering at an ARBA (American Rare Breed Association) Tournament of Champions. Joining these PONs are their "cousins," the Chart Polski and the Owczarek Podhalanski, also known as the Owczarek Tatrazanski, or Tatra.

Wies Kennels. Encouraged that others were attempting to reestablish this wonderful breed, she purchased two puppies from the Babia Wies Kennels, Dukat and Diuna. She then retrieved Smok back to her kennel—the year was 1955. Next, she acquired a young, white, bob-tailed bitch from Krakow. Her name was Wiga and she is believed to have been the link with early PONs of Planta and Milanow, probably related to the pair of PONs that survived World War II with Ms. W. Zoltowska.

FATHER OF THE BREED

Smok was an excellent dog, perfectly anatomically built, with a wonderful temperament. Dr. Hryniewicz considered Smok the epitome of the breed. Smok was the standard by which she bred, before there was a standard, and the type to be emulated by PON breeders for generations to come. The standard, which was written by Mrs. M. Dubrowinowa, was accepted by the Polish Kennel Club in 1959.

Dr. Hryniewicz bred three litters in 1956—two litters by Smok and

Smok z Kordegardy. By the end of World War II, the Polski Owczarek Nizinny was near extinction. It was because of this extraordinary dog and his owner Dr. Danuta Hryniewicz that the breed came to receive the recognition it rightly deserves.

highly homozygous—passed all his virtues to his progeny."

Dr. Hryniewicz had requests for puppies from all over Poland. She sent puppies from every litter to work with sheep on farms in her area and later took some back to her kennel to breed, to ensure that the breed's utility ability remained intact.

In 1958, Dr. Hryniewicz bred her first litter with full pedigrees. By 1969, Kordegardy Kennels had produced 150 puppies, and 31 of them became champions. Some of the noteworthy PONs of yesteryear are: Harfa, who became the mother of the first international champion—Amok Moniek; Inkluz and Iwa; Lider, who was the sire of the famous Int. Ch. Doman; Assan; Garda Wtora; Duda, mother of Ch. Witez, who sired a well-known dog named Ch. Gwarek z Psiego Raju; Ch. Szelma; Ch. Lubek; and Ch. Rola. (All are Kordegardy dogs unless otherwise noted.)

According to attorney Lubomir Smyczynski, a recognized authority, judge, and consultant on the breed who has written a number of articles published all over the world about the PON, it took 15 years after World War II to get the breed established and have several top quality dogs for

Diuna and one litter by Smok and Wiga. Smok sired ten litters from 1956 to 1959. Of necessity, there was extensive inbreeding. Smok was used with his daughters and granddaughters and produced the kind of dogs breeders and farmers were looking for. In Dr. Hryniewicz's own words:

"In that time (in the fifties) I used rather strong inbreeding in my kennel. I was lucky that it didn't give any bad results. I think I owe it all to Smok, who—being breeding. The first international dog show where a significant number of PONs were presented was the World Dog Show in Czechoslovakia in 1965. Nine Polish Lowland Sheepdogs were shown, and they all received excellent marks. Two were awarded CACIBs (Certificate of Aptitude for Championship of International Beauty), and two received Reserve CACIBs. After 1970, the breed became noticeably more popular in Poland, and many new breeders

Int., Wd., Pol. Ch. Malwina z Kordegardy, by Kompan z Kordegardy ex Drumla z Kordegardy.

Dr. Hryniewicz and some of her PONs z Kordegardy: the well-known Smok, Nerpa, Kuma, and Smok's grandson Arak Greps. Photo by H. Skalska.

joined the ranks. Most started with Kordegardy dogs, some with bitches of unknown pedigree. By 1975, there were 66 PON kennels in Poland, most with only one to three bitches. Several PONs were shown at the World Dog Show in Budapest in 1971. The Federation Cynologique Internationale (FCI) officially recognized the breed in 1959 and accepted changes in the standard in 1963 and 1973.

Ch. Lechsinska's Krol Wladyslaw, by Elzbieta's Beau ex Ch. Elzbieta's Rola Lenska. Owner, Cindy Czerechowicz. Handler, Laurie Pearson.

Standard for the Polski Owczarek Nizinny

FCI Registered Number 251a, 1973

GENERAL APPEARANCE AND CHARACTER

The Polski Owczarek Nizinny is a medium-sized dog, cobby, strong, and muscular, with a long, thick coat and an easy, smooth gait. It is resistant to unfavorable conditions, lively but self-controlled, watchful, bright, clever, and perceptive with an excellent memory.

HEIGHT AT SHOULDERS

Dog, 45-50 cm. (18-20 in.); Bitch, 42-47 cm. (16½-18 in.)

PROPORTIONS

Height 9/ Length 10.

TYPE

It is not desirable to diminish the size below the standard and make the dog delicate, as it should keep the character of a working dog.

UTILITY

It is easy to train, as it works as a shepherd and as a watchdog. Transferred to town, it is a very good companion dog. Its coat, when well groomed, makes it look smart and attractive.

Seven–month–old Przemek's Huxley, by Premier Oligarchia ex Inbred Lapowka, exhibiting a natural stance. Photo by M. Supronowicz.

HEAD

General Appearance—
Proportioned, medium sized, not too heavy, with profuse hair on the forehead, cheeks, and chin, which makes it look bigger than it actually is. The ratio between its mouth and skull is 1:1, or the muzzle may be a little shorter. **Skull**—Moderately broad, slightly domed. The forehead furrow and occiput palpable. **Stop**—Distinctly marked. **Mouth**—The top line of the muzzle is straight, jaws strong. **Nose**—A big, blunt nose with wide nostrils, as dark as possible within the particular color. **Lips**—Tightly closed, with edges of the same color as the nose. **Teeth**—Strong, level, or scissor. **Eyes**—Medium size, of lively, penetrating gaze, oval, not

Bozena Borkowska, daughter of Dr. Tomasz Borkowski, one of the authors, working with one of the PONs at Elzbieta Kennels. This PON has good front movement.

Huxley demonstrating good movement and reach. When viewed from the side, the PON's body appears rectangular rather than square. Photo by M. Supronowicz.

protruding. Color, hazel or brown. The edges of the lids must be as dark as possible. **Ears**—Medium sized, lively, heart-shaped, large at the base, set moderately high, drooping, their fore edge tightly set against the cheek.

NECK

Strong, muscular, of medium length, without any dewlap, held rather horizontally.

BODY

General Appearance—
Silhouette rectangular rather than square. **Withers**—Distinctively marked. **Back**—Even, muscular, loins broad, well bound. **Croup**—Short, tightly cut. **Chest**—Deep, ribs moderately cut, neither flat nor barrel-like. **Belly**—Slightly drawn up.

TAIL

Innately short or rudimentary, or very shortly docked.

FOREQUARTERS

General Appearance—As seen from the front and side, straight, a well-balanced stance due to a strong skeleton. **Shoulders**—Broad, of medium length, slant, well-bound, and muscular. **Metacarp**—Slightly slant in relation to the forearm. **Feet**—Oval, toes tight, slightly arched, with hard pads, claws short, possibly dark.

HINDQUARTERS

General Appearance—Well angled, straight as seen from behind. **Thigh**—Broad, well muscled. **Hock**—Distinct.

GAIT

Mostly smooth walking pace or trot. The dog is often an ambler.

SKIN

Tight, without any folds.

COAT

The whole body is covered with a long, dense, shaggy thick coat, with a soft, dense undercoat. The long hair covers the eyes characteristically. Slightly wavy coat admissible.

COLOR

Every color and piebald allowed.

FAULTS

Head—Round, apple shaped.
Profile—The topline of the muzzle convex or concave.
Nose and Lips—Lack of pigment.

SKC Ch. Inbred Lapowka, by Ch. Palasz z Wielgowa ex Leta z Kordegardy. Lapowka is the dam of one of the most-titled PONs in the world: Ch. of the Americas, Int., So.Am., P.R., SKC Ch. Elzbieta's Polski Duma. Photo by T. Borkowski.

Teeth—Faulty dentition.
Eyes—Light yellow or jackdaw eye.
Ears—Set too high.
Back—Weak or roach back.
Chest—Greyhound or barrel-shaped.
Neck—Held too high.
Loins—Feeble.
Tail—If not docked, it should not be curled over the back.
Legs—Incorrect stance, too long.
Coat—Curly or short, without undercoat.
Character—Nervous, cowardly, phlegmatic.

Klon Akribeia minding the sheep at Elzbieta Kennels. The Polski Owczarek Nizinny has served as a working dog since the 16th century. Photo by B. Augustowski.

Comments about the Standard for the PON

The first standard of the Polski Owczarek Nizinny was written by Maria Dubrowinowa and accepted by the Polish Kennel Club and the FCI in 1959. This standard was changed slightly by the Polish Kennel Club and these proposed modifications were accepted by the FCI in 1963 and 1973. In 1989, the PON Club of Poland recommended and proposed the following changes to the accepted standard:

Height at Shoulders: Dog, 18 inches to 20 inches (45 to 50 cm.). Bitch, 17 inches to 19 inches (42 to 47 cm.).

Tail: Tail cannot be longer than two vertebrae.

Feet: Oval, toes tight.

INTERPRETATION OF THE CURRENT STANDARD

The standard describes the ideal PON, which exists only in the imagination. This means that each of us has a somewhat different conception of the ideal PON. The standard provides a "blueprint" to which we should endeavor to breed and by which PONs are judged in the conformation ring. The following comments and discussion do not

Ali, Esther, and Wally enjoying the great outdoors. All PONs must regularly be given the opportunity for fresh air and exercise. Ali and Esther owned by Nancy Gardzelewski; Wally owned by Cindy Czerechowicz.

A PON pup and his little pal getting acquainted. PONs and youngsters can get along well together.

an excellent memory. Though these are true attributes of the PON, it is important to realize that the PON needs a dominant master and good consistent training from the time it is very young. If this is not provided, the PON will tend to dominate its master.

The PON needs close contact with people. If left in a kennel crate for long periods of time, the dog will become either suspicious and shy or wild and aggressive, overreacting to various situations. It is very easy to train a PON for good behavior, and they are so intelligent that a little bit of work by its master will go a long way and benefit the entire family. PONs have no problem accepting the needs of an entire family.

Head

The typical PON head is large in proportion to its body. The head should not be too heavy, but the abundant amount of hair makes it look larger than its actual size.

The standard states that the ratio between the mouth and skull is 1:1. This means that the length of the muzzle from nose to stop should be equal in length to the distance from the stop to occiput. However, according to a study conducted by Mr. T. Krystek of show PONs in 1984, it has been established that the muzzle is actually slightly longer than the length of the skull. According to his study, the ratio of muzzle to skull in males is an average of 1 to .95; in females an average of 1 to .96. It is extremely rare to find a PON with a muzzle

refer to any particular dog, but to the standard.

General Appearance

Males as well as females should be as close to the maximum height for the standard as possible. They should be strong, well built, and muscular, with a large head that is not carried too high. The dog should have a long, straight, thick coat over the entire body, with the head heavily covered so that the eyes cannot be seen.

Temperament

The standard states that the PON is clever and perceptive, with

shorter than the length of the skull.

The skull should be broad, and almost flat. It should never be apple shaped or round, which is considered to be a fault. When touching the stop you should notice a pronounced indentation, but the stop is never as pronounced as in round-skulled breeds.

The bite should be scissor or level. A PON with slightly irregular dentition should not be penalized, but a significant overbite or underbite is not acceptable. According to the PON Club of Poland, the PON is expected to have full dentition, as it is a utility breed. Full dentition consists of the following: 6 incisors in both upper and lower jaw; 2 canines, one on each side, in upper and lower jaw; 8 premolars, 4 on each side in both upper and lower jaw; 4 molars in the upper jaw, 2 on each side; 6 molars in the lower jaw, 3 on each side.

The teeth should be white and strong. If the canine teeth in the lower jaw are not in front of the upper canine teeth, the lower jaw is too narrow, which is considered a fault.

The nose should be large and black or brown, depending upon the coat color of the dog. A pink nose or a nose partially lacking pigmentation should be penalized.

The eyes should be of medium size, never too large or prominent, and slightly oval or almond shaped. They should be dark in color. Most PONs have dark or

Some of Tom Wason's and Loana Shields's "Polish kids." In overall appearance, the PON is strong and cobby.

hazel-colored eyes. This conforms to the standard. Dogs with lighter colored coats may have lighter colored eyes. However, if the eyes are too light in color, it is considered a fault. The eye rims should be darker than the eyes, and black pigmentation is preferred. A condition in which the eyelid rolls inward is referred to as entropion, which is considered in many breeds to be hereditary. The presence of entropion of the eye must be considered a fault, as it possibly can result in corneal scarring.

Ears should be set moderately high, but not too high. They are of medium size in proportion to the head and should be fully covered with long hair.

Neck

The neck should be muscular and rather thick. It should be broad, never narrow. The standard states that the neck is held rather horizontally; however, in the show ring the neck should be carried slightly higher than the topline in order to give the dog a look of class and elegance. The neck should be heavily coated, particularly in the male. The skin on the neck should be tight, without wrinkles.

Body

The back should be neither too long nor too short for proper balance and movement. The body shape should be rectangular rather than square. The standard states that the ratio of height to length is 9 to 10, which means that the height of the dog at the withers should equal 9/10ths its length. However, the study previously referred to in this chapter conducted by Mr. T.

Breeders on both sides of the Atlantic have worked diligently to perpetuate the PON's herding abilities.

Krystek found that proportions for the male were actually an average of 9.63 to 10 and 9.55 to 10 in females. This seems to indicate that even very long-bodied PONs may be acceptable.

The PON Club of Poland prefers a well-balanced PON that is not too long in length. Withers should be well pronounced and broad. The chest should be deep and broad. The topline is level. The loin is well muscled and broad, creating a dog that is and gives the appearance o f being strong. The croup should be slightly cut, but only to a small degree.

Tail

The tail should be short, set low, and no longer than two vertebrae. It should not change the shape of the body.

There has been considerable

Ideally, a PON's head will be large and heavily covered with fur. The nose also should be large. Its coloration should be black or brown, depending on the dog's coat color.

Puppy "Pietno," aka Jigs, practicing his herding tactics on the family kitty. PONs and cats can get along well if they are introduced early on and are properly supervised. Owner, Carl Davi.

controversy over the tail. The standard states that the tail is innately short or very shortly docked. The standard provides under "Faults" that a dog's tail that is not short or docked should not be carried over the back.

Mr. Jorg Haufschild, a German, began showing PONs with long tails in German and Polish show rings. As a result, the PONs with long tails were expelled from the West German PON Club and formed a separate club.

In an average litter of PON puppies, some are born completely without tails, some with full-length tails, and most with varying lengths in between these two. It is unusual to find a whole litter of PONs with perfect long tails.

A typical PON "smile." The Polski Owczarek Nizinny is a bright, clever, and perceptive dog.

In many of the European countries, tail docking is not permissible. Consequently, there is a need for the Polish Kennel Club to address this aspect of the standard and to consider "tails that are not docked." In the U.S., we follow the Polish and FCI regulations.

Initially it was believed that a single gene determined the length of the tail. Many years ago, it was also thought that the "bob-tail" was associated with a lethal gene. It was, therefore, recommended that a male born naturally bob-tailed not be bred to a naturally born bob-tailed mother. Every attempt was made to breed a dog born with a short tail only to dogs born with long tails.

It has since been determined that this theory was incorrect. Modern research has established that the length of the tail is not controlled by a single gene, but by several different genes.

A study conducted in 1988 resulted in major changes in these theories. In 1988, a study conducted by G. Pindera focused on the possible influence of bob-tailed genes on the average number of puppies born in a litter. This study showed that the average number of puppies in a litter was significantly higher in those litters where naturally bob-tailed puppies appeared. These litters also contained a significantly higher number of puppy bitches.

Dr. Danuta Hryniewicz, who was the largest breeder of PONs in Poland for many years, said that she often bred bob-tailed mothers to bob-tailed fathers with no ill effects. These breedings regularly resulted in very nice large litters. Although Polish breeders no longer practice the old rule of breeding bob-tails to long-tailed dogs, the PON Club of Poland still prefers documentation of a puppy's tail length at birth.

Forequarters

The shoulder blades should not be too broad or long and should be covered with heavy strong muscle. The shoulder blade should be well laid back, which means that the upper part of this broad bone lies next to the dog's spine at a backward slant. This causes the lower end of the shoulder blade to automatically slope diagonally downward and forward to the chest, where it connects to the upper foreleg bone, the humerus. The position of the shoulder blade on the spine is often referred to as a 45-degree angle. The humerus and elbows should be close to the body, but not too tight. The preference is for a deep brisket containing the breast bone. Forelegs should be heavy in bone and when viewed from the front, should be parallel. The feet should be oval, thick, and compact, with the front feet larger than the rear feet. Excessively light-boned feet are penalized.

Hindquarters

The hindquarters should be large, heavily boned, and well

Happy Holidays. Donna Gray with Ch. Elzbieta's Polish Jazz and Elzbieta's Malgosia.

muscled. The angulation of rear legs from back to heel when viewed from the rear should appear parallel and straight when the dog is standing or moving.

Coat

This is a very important aspect of the standard regardless of the sex or coat color of the dog. The standard requires that the dog be double coated with a soft, dense undercoat, well covered by a long, dense, thick, shaggy, and reasonably straight coat. It is not unusual for a PON's coat to measure 10 to 12 inches in length. In general, males tend to have better coats than females.

It is desirable that the type and quality of the coat be the same over the entire dog. Occasionally you will see a PON that has two different types of coat, with the front portion conforming to the standard but the rear portion less coated, curly, standing up, or not as thick. This gives the impression that the hindquarters are higher, weaker, or not balanced with the forequarters.

Dogs exhibited in the show ring

Ch. Ponwood's Esther Ofarim at one year of age. Ideally, the PON coat is long, straight, and thick over the entire body. Owner, Nancy Gardzelewski.

are required to be shown in a natural state. This means that dogs must not be trimmed, and in particular the face is not to be trimmed. The PON in the show ring should look natural, with an emphasis towards shagginess as required by the standard. Grooming preparation with the use of scissors or thinning shears is not recommended, and the dog cannot be visibly trimmed. Dogs are occasionally seen in the ring today prepared by professional handlers or groomers in a manner similar to that of the Bearded Collie. This appearance is incorrect for the PON.

According to the standard, all coat colors are acceptable. However, this does not mean you will find all coat colors in the PON breed. The most common coat colors are white with black, gray, or sandy patches, and gray with white or chocolate. Very rarely are they all white, all black, or black and tan. Coat colors of brindle, blue, blue merle, mahogany, and several others have not been seen in this breed as of yet.

Most PONs carry a dominant "fading" factor genetically, which results in puppies being born darker in coat color than they will appear as adults, with the exception of those puppies born white. Most puppies' coats will begin to lighten between the ages of 8 to 12 weeks, with changes in coat color first becoming evident at the roots of the outer coat and becoming more noticeable as the coat grows. Coat color in dogs containing this factor generally reaches its lightest stage at about

Brunek z Elzbieta, by Pol. Ch. Apasz z Bankowcow ex Krymka z Kordegardy. Brunek is the sire of some of the top show PONs in the US. Photo by Cle Francis, *Dog World*.

12 to 18 months and then begins to darken to the dog's mature coat color, but the PONs carrying this trait will not return to the color of their puppy coat. These dogs continue to change intensity of coat color many times during their lives. Because of this fading factor, dogs born black and white often become gray and white or silver and white at adulthood. There are a few PONs that have remained black or black and silver into adulthood, but this is extremely rare.

If a puppy is born dark brown, it will be chocolate. Chocolate PONs have brown noses, eye rims, and lips. The iris color is also lighter amber rather than hazel.

The graying, or fading, factor will change the chocolate to beige, but the pigmentation must stay brown. A pink or partial pigmentation of nose and eye rims or mouth is unacceptable with any coat color.

A genetic color pattern is not definitely established in this breed, but it is believed that there are some similarities with the Bearded Collie coat color pattern.

Movement

The PON is a utility dog, and the standard dictates a smooth walking or trotting pace. Both front and rear movement are equally important.

A dog with the correct shoulder

PONs love to work. Here, Kontrapunkt Ceramika tends sheep. Photo by Broman.

Bozena Borkowska with Elzbieta's Claudius, by Brunek z Elzbieta ex Branka z Kordegardy. It is said that PONs have excellent memories ar d will long remember instances of being treated kindly—or unkindly. Photo by B. Augustowski.

From Elzbieta Kennels: Awans z Kordegardy, Krymka z Kordegardy, Brunek z Elzbieta, Anetka z Elzbieta, and Elzbieta's Pan Vladek, Betty and Caz Augustowski's first PON. Photo by B. Augustowski.

Margaret Supronowicz, one of the authors, with Mutsnah z Elzbieta and Awans z Kordegardy. Photo by T. Borkowski.

angulation is capable of swinging his front legs forward with great reach of stride, extending out before his body in a long flat arch. This stride propels the body forward, rather than upward, with less fatigue. A dog without this shoulder angulation has a much shorter front stride and is unable to propel himself forward without much greater effort and many more steps to cover the same distance. When viewed from the front, the legs should move parallel from the elbows to the pasterns. "Toeing in" is considered rather natural, while "toeing out" is considered a fault.

A dog with good rear angulation is able to bring his legs forward like a compressor. The greatest source of a dog's forward drive is derived from the backward swing of its leg, aided by the longer muscle that supports the bone. When viewed from behind, the back legs should be parallel to each other and not too close. Common movement faults in PONs are rear gaits that are too close and cow hocks, with cow hocks being the more common of the two.

In general, the PON exhibits good or very good front movement, with some problem in rear movement. Correct hindquarter structure and movement appear to be relatively rare in the PON. As the PON is a working breed, any fault handicapping free movement must be heavily penalized.

Faults

In addition to faults specifically listed in the standard, all faults designated in the *Nicholas Guide* to Dog Judging and The New Step by R. Page Elliott should be considered as such and undesirable.

Balance

All factors considered, the most important aspect in evaluating a PON is balance. Balance is dependent upon proportion between size of head, length of neck, depth of chest, and length of legs and body, each to the other. Balance is also required between front and rear during movement.

The PON is a rear trotter, but not in the same manner as the German Shepherd. When first introduced to the show ring after World War II, Polish judges expected the PON to move as a German Shepherd, but PON movement is entirely different. Due to its body structure and anatomy, PON movement is of a completely different type, without the reach and drive exhibited by the German Shepherd.

Above: Pan Vladek, by Bundz z Starego Lupkowa ex Fajerka z Kordegardy, and Krymka z Kordegardy, by Kaduk Ogrodek Magdy ex Plaza z Kordegardy. Krymka was the Augustowskis' first PON from Poland. She was the mother or grandmother of seven of the first ten US champions.

Beautiful headstudy of Ch. of the Americas, Int., So.Am., P.R., SKC Ch. Mutsnah z Elzbieta, owned by Betty Augustowski.

Judging the PON

Many American judges have difficulty evaluating PONs in the show ring because the PON is a rare breed, and little educational literature is available here to clarify the standard.

A similar situation existed in Poland after World War II, when no written standard on the PON had been adopted. After the first standard was published, most herding judges expected to see many similarities between the PON and the German Shepherd, which was very popular at that time, especially in movement. This was not beneficial to the breed.

The PON differs somewhat from other herding breeds. It is not a small Old English Sheepdog and it is not a Bearded Collie. Judges carry a great responsibility and play an important role in shaping the future of this magnificent breed, as show decisions, points, and certificates are having tremendous influence in the development of the PONs in this country. It is important that a judge feel the breed carefully to be able to distinguish it from breeds that appear similar, and in order to be able to recognize the best specimen of the PON competing among others.

It is not uncommon for an exhibitor to approach a judge to request an evaluation of his dog

Best of Breed competition at the first National Specialty in Washington, DC. Attending shows will give you the opportunity to see what qualities breeders are breeding for, and the chance to make new friends that share your interest in the PON. Photo by T. Borkowski.

after the breed competition is completed. A judge should be prepared to give his opinion, and comments should always be forthright. Such comments should include all positive attributes of the particular dog, but all faults should be mentioned as well. Even the most outstanding champions have some faults. This type of exchange between judges and exhibitors benefits the breed as well as the exhibitor.

It is important to remember that the PON is still a rare breed and should be judged positively for as many good points as it has, without emphasis on the bad, except for disqualifying faults. When judging PONs, it is

SKC Ch. Inbred Lapowka, who took Best of Breed at the first National Specialty of the American Pol. Owczarek Nizinny Club (APONC).

necessary not only to look at each dog carefully and from every possible angle, but also to keep in mind the future of the breed when making awards.

To judge to everyone's liking and satisfaction is very difficult, and most of the time it is impossible. There is an old German proverb, "He who is a judge between two friends loses one of them." A judge must make his decisions without the help of anyone, and his responsibilities are limited to the day of the show and time of judging. PONs are shaggy, hairy dogs, and the ringside spectators do not know what a judge finds during his careful examination of a dog. The spectators see only a dog with a beautiful, excellent long coat.

In judging the breed, it is important to keep in mind that PONs are primarily utility-herding dogs, and they have proven to be good workers. They are not only great obedience competitors, but great family companions as well. They are strong, muscled, and superb guard and personal protection dogs.

As a judge, do not be surprised to encounter in the ring a PON that is not flexible, cooperative, and easy to walk around the ring, as they generally do not show well for professional handlers. From the time that the dogs enter the ring, pay attention to their behavior. If the PON is shy, spooked, afraid, vicious, or shows any signs that it may not be examined in the normal way, it should be considered "not typical."

After watching movement, judges like to see PONs in a posed standing position. PONs do not require tables. They should be stacked on the floor or ground. PONs are robust and muscular, proportioned with a large head and big nostrils. Because they are long-coated dogs, they must be examined very carefully.

Important aspects in judging are proportion of the head, teeth, depth of chest, pronounced withers, configuration of croup, formation of legs, and coat texture.

Common faults are:

1. Head too small (apple-shaped head)
2. Stop insufficiently pronounced
3. Light eyes
4. Weak and narrow jaw
5. Soft topline
6. Arched loins
7. Rear quarters too narrow or weak
8. Cow hocks
9. Lack of free action, short steps
10. Soft and woolly coat

The dog in the show ring cannot be visibly scissored. It should be shown as natural as possible, without any visible trimming. Coat coloring or artificial preparation should be penalized.

Before making a final decision, the condition of the PON should also be considered. Remember that PONs are great eaters, so they tend to be stout. If there is only one PON in the ring, he should be given as much time as would be given many competitors. The standard does not have disqualifying faults, but PONs are supposed to be judged according to the general show rules for disqualifications.

Wesolych Swiat (Merry Christmas)! from Ali and the Gardzelewski family.

Disqualifications are:

1. Lameness
2. Deafness
3. Blindness
4. Monorchidism
5. Cryptorchidism
6. Spayed or castrated
7. Abnormal behavior
8. Viciousness
9. Shy or timid temperament

The same champion PON before (above) and after (below) its bath. A PON's coat should be allowed to grow naturally; it should never be clipped or sculpted. Photos by T. Borkowski.

Grooming

BRUSH THAT COAT

A well-groomed PON has a long, dense, luxurious thick coat with a soft undercoat. If you want your PON to look nice all the time, you must be prepared to brush his hair religiously and keep him clean. A puppy should be introduced to grooming and bathing procedures at an early age. You can begin brushing your puppy when he seems comfortable in his new surroundings. This is another new experience for him, so make it as pleasant as possible. You should have a positive attitude towards grooming; it should be fun for the dog to be groomed and receive personal attention from his owner. Never start to groom when you are feeling tired or rushed. You have to have the time to be gentle and patient with your dog. Ideally, brushing a young puppy once or twice daily for short

Some dog owners can't resist gussying up their pets, and PON owners are no exception. Ali and Esther seem pleased with a Halloween theme. Owner, Nancy Gardzelewski.

sessions is good training. Hold the pup in your lap and brush his entire body, including the feet and face. Take special care around the eyes. You want the puppy to accept grooming as an inevitable, not unpleasant, part of life. Young puppies have very short hair that does not mat. You will not have that problem until your PON is eight or nine months old. When he gets too big for your lap, you can groom him on a table, with the dog standing or lying on his side.

TANGLES TAKE TIME

Caring for the double-coated adult PON requires special attention. If the coat is badly matted, you must break up as many of the mats as possible by hand before brushing; otherwise,

A PON being groomed for show. Even if you are not interested in showing, your PON must be groomed regularly to prevent the build-up of unsightly mats, which can also cause discomfort.

the coat will be ripped out. Try to gently pull the mats apart with your thumb and forefinger. As a last resort, if you absolutely cannot pull a mat apart, use the scissors, slicing lengthwise to split the mat (one blade in a sawing motion—cut, if sawing doesn't work for you). Never cut crosswise against the direction of the hair growth. You can cut a little more freely (where it won't show) in the friction areas: under/behind ears, between toes, armpits, and inner thighs. Being as careful as possible, brush the dog thoroughly. Remove any remaining mats but be careful to remove as little hair as possible.

Use a good pin brush, not a slicker brush, which will remove the undercoat and leave your PON looking like a Bearded Collie. There are many good brushes on the market, but make sure you choose a flexible brush.

With the dog on a table, either standing or lying on one side then the other, start brushing from the head, then the neck, the body, and the legs. Brush from the skin to the end of the hair. Don't use a comb on a dirty coat. A steel comb should be used only on a clean coat without mats to uncover any mats you may have missed.

EYES, EARS, TOES, ETC.

After the dog is thoroughly brushed, attention should be given to eyes, ears, teeth, toes, and anal glands. Most long-haired dogs will get "sleep" in the inner corners of their eyes. This matter must be removed frequently. If it should accumulate into a large mass that is difficult to budge, soften it with a wet towel first and remove. Inner-ear hair and hair between the toes should be plucked out or trimmed with blunt-end scissors. Keeping the inside of the ears free of hair and dirt will prevent irritation and inflammation. After removing the

checked carefully to ensure that the puppy is losing his puppy teeth normally. Sometimes, the new canine teeth come in before the puppy canine teeth have dropped out. You can try giving the puppy something hard to bite on, or simply remove the baby tooth so that the permanent tooth will grow in properly. PONs

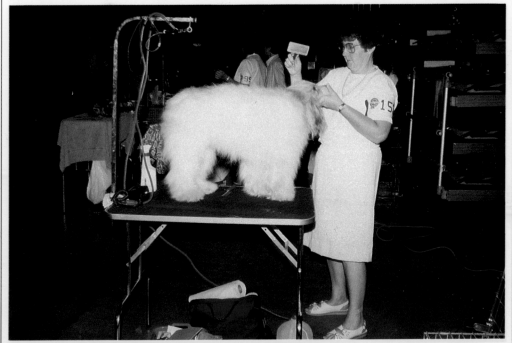

Finishing touches before show time. A good grooming table will help to facilitate grooming your PON.

hair, clean out the ear canal with a cotton swab softened with hydrogen peroxide. If you can see any irritation in the ear, you can use a little ear cream. If you detect a bad odor from the ear or see a brown or black discharge in the ear, or if the dog shakes his head incessantly, it may be some kind of infection that requires veterinary attention.

The teeth of puppies between four and six months should be

usually do not have problems with their teeth. They do not lose their teeth too early and enjoy chewing on hard foods, such as dried biscuits, which will keep their teeth clean. There are a great variety of Nylabone products available that veterinarians recommend as safe and healthy for dogs or puppies to chew on. These Nylabone Pooch Pacifiers usually don't splinter, chip, or break off in large chunks; instead,

The PON's coat can be one of a number of different colors, each of which is attractive in its own way.

they are frizzled by a dog's chewing action, and this creates a toothbrush-like surface that cleanses the teeth and massages the gums. If the teeth are a little yellow, you can also use a toothbrush with toothpaste for dogs. In cases of bad neglect, scaling a dog's teeth can help to save or salvage affected teeth. Your veterinarian can perform this procedure.

The frequency of cutting the toenails of PONs depends on the type of surface the dog comes in contact with during his exercise periods. If your dog spends his days on the grass of your backyard, his nails will need to be trimmed as often as once every month; however, if your PON spends most of his time on concrete or another hard surface, or if he is a working dog, you won't need to cut his nails very often, possibly not at all. When cutting the nails, care must be taken not to cut into the quick. If the nail is white, it is easy to see where the blood vessels are, but if the nail is black it is more difficult. You can cut a little bit at a time until you see a white or black dot. Stop at that point so you will not cut into the vein. If you accidentally cut too far, you can stop the bleeding by administering a small amount of styptic powder. Guillotine-style nail clippers are available for use on dogs.

The last thing before bathing is to check the dog's anal glands and remove the hair that may obstruct the anal area. The anal glands excrete a lubricant that enables the dog to easily expel the contents of the rectum.

Sometimes this fluid builds up, and the excess must be expelled by hand. With the thumb and forefinger, take hold of the grape-sized protrusions on either side of the rectum and press firmly. A small amount of thick, foul-smelling liquid will be expelled. The dog may experience a moment of discomfort, but the procedure is not painful. If you are reluctant to tend to this matter, ask your groomer or veterinarian to check your dog's anal glands.

THE BATH

You can start bathing your dog after he has had all of his vaccinations. It is easy to bathe a little dog; this can be done every two to three weeks at first and then monthly. The frequency of puppy baths is more for training than for cleanliness or coat conditioning.

Use a good dog shampoo. If you prefer, you can use one especially formulated for color, i.e., black or white. Wet the dog down with warm water from the rear end first to slowly accustom him to the feeling. When the dog is wet all over, work in the shampoo with your fingers. One or two sudsings are generally enough. Rinse thoroughly, then condition. Rinse thoroughly again. Be as careful when washing your dog's head as you would be when shampooing a child's hair.

Elzbieta's Ciena, owned by Mary Von Drehle. The PON's ancestry most likely includes the Puli and other rugged longhaired herding dogs.

BLOW DRYING

After the dog is rinsed, you can towel dry him by squeezing out the excess water, not by rubbing. If you leave your PON to dry naturally, he will mat more easily. Blow drying is recommended for maintaining the coat at its best and it is essential for a show coat. Brush out the coat while drying, ideally on a table. To prevent any burning, make sure that the temperature is not too hot, and don't hold the dryer too close to the dog or keep it on one spot too long. It is better to dry the dog part by part, that is, one leg completely dry, then the next leg completely dry, than to partially dry all over. You have to slowly accustom your PON to the noise and heat of the blow dryer. Sometimes young puppies can be a little afraid. Again, start with the hind legs, with the dog standing or lying on one side, then the other. Brush the coat away from you, parting and layering a section at a time. This will give the coat a fuller effect. Remember to praise your dog constantly for being so tolerant.

If you want your dog to look like a Polski Owczarek Nizinny, his coat must be allowed to grow naturally, without *any* clipping or sculpting. Minimal trimming in the following areas is sensible. The hair between the pads should be trimmed with scissors, but only from the bottom of the foot, not around the foot. Also, the area around the anus and the area around the penis on male dogs can be trimmed for cleanliness. Even if you have trouble keeping the eyes clean, the hair should not be cut under the eyes—this will spoil the PON's whole expression.

Never cut the hair around the area of the eyes. If for any reason you want to restrain it, e.g., at mealtime, use a barrette or rubber band, as seen here on "Cosi," formally known as Ch. Cosmos Tarok Bator.

CLIPPING

If you do not care to keep your PON in long coat, without the necessity of constant grooming and brushing, you can clip your dog down. He will certainly not resemble a sheepdog, but he will be clean and the hair will grow back in time. In previous centuries, when PONs were used exclusively for herding, it was believed that shepherds sheared their dogs along with the sheep. It does not permanently damage the coat to clip it; it will grow out evenly if it is clipped properly. A #10-size blade works well if you have some experience in clipping dogs. If not, a grooming salon should be considered.

SHOW GROOMING

To prepare your PON for the show ring, you should try to make him look as close to the standard as possible. The PON is proportional, rectangular, not too short, and not too long. It is a dog with a medium-sized head that looks larger than it actually is because of the profuse hair on the forehead, cheeks, and chin. The coat is not supposed to be wiry, hard, silky nor woolly, but thick, long, and dense.

To keep your PON in show condition, you must bathe him more frequently than once a month. Be careful while brushing to take out as little hair as possible, always using the pin brush, not the slicker, which will remove undercoat.

All basic grooming and bathing procedures already discussed are the same for the show or pet PON, with a few additional steps for the show dog. To protect and condition its show coat, the show PON can be "put in oil." A suggested solution to use would be two to four tablespoons of conditioner and two to four tablespoons of lanolin-oil preparation with a quart of warm water, using one of the following methods.

Method 1

In the tub, after bathing and thoroughly rinsing out soap, completely saturate the coat with

PON littermates. One is in clipped coat; the other is in full coat. Photo by T. Borkowski.

Grooming a PON for show takes a lot of time and effort, but knowing that your PON will look his best in the ring makes it all worthwhile.

the conditioning preparation. Squeeze, blot out excess, then blow dry, brushing as you dry. It will take longer to dry the coat with the oil in it.

Method 2

Bathe, condition, and dry normally. Within a day or two, apply the oil by spraying it on one section of the hair at a time. Do not soak the coat. Dry with the blow dryer, but do not brush the oil mixture all the way to the ends of the hairs. Mats form mostly near the skin; this is where the treatment is most helpful. Also, since oil tends to attract and hold dirt, it is better to leave the more exposed ends of the coat free of oil.

Method 1 is best if the coat is especially dry or damaged. Method 2 is more for maintenance. The dog need not be put in oil every time it is bathed, but it should be done as frequently as possible.

Prior to a show, bathe your dog one or two days before, without the oil treatment. While blow drying, keep in mind the standard. If your dog is a little high in the rear, for instance, blow dry just on the withers and behind the withers against the hair growth, while blow drying with the hair on the loin part to make it look as low as possible. The object is to have a smooth, straight topline. Before the show, you can use a little hair spray to keep the hair where you want it.

For a wavy or fine coat, very lightly spray overall (one side at a time) with a mixture of eight parts water, one part cream rinse, and one or two drops of lanolin. Blow dry while brushing—this is a mini version of after-bath grooming. If any new mats have formed, pull them out carefully.If your dog has a white or light-colored, full straight coat, wetting is not necessary before ring time. Powder the coat lightly with corn starch and brush it out completely. Chalk on the legs and face will dry and whiten hair for last-minute touches. Remember that you want the legs and the head to look as full as possible. Just before going in the ring, brush the feet and lower legs

This young PON sports a poodle–clip style. If your PON's coat is clipped correctly, it will grow out evenly.

upward to fluff. Shake each leg— the coat will fall downward while keeping the look of fullness.

Keeping a PON in show condition takes a lot of work. You have to be very careful about mats and foreign bodies in the coat. Promptly remove any leaves, burrs, or dirt that may be picked up during exercise periods. Protect the long hairs of his ears when he is eating by using a smaller, deeper bowl. To prevent excessive hair covering the eyes during exercising or obedience training, you can make a knot on the top of the head using a ribbon or a rubber band.

SKC Ch. Inbred Lapowka, by Ch. Palasz z Wielgowa ex Leta z Kordegardy. Photo by T. Borkowski.

Showing Your PON

Many PON owners presently exhibiting their dogs in the U.S. purchased their first dog with no intentions of doing so. Then, due to their fascination with and love for the breed, they became involved in obedience and conformation classes, and ultimately took on the challenge of entering the show ring.

Should you decide to accept this challenge, you must realize that this is not an easy breed to show. Bonding and socialization of the PON are very important, as is true with all herding breeds. The PON is generally a one-family dog. It has been said that "If you work and play with them, they will die for you." If ignored, they will withdraw.

The PON becomes very attached to its owner and does not find the idea of being "on stage" appealing. If you are interested in showing your dog, you must take advantage of handling classes to obtain good results. Because of the bond between the PON and its master, it does not perform well for a professional handler, no matter how well trained it may be. In general, the PON will perform much better for its owner than for an unknown person. This requires the PON owner to become skilled in handling his or her own dog, as poor handling can give a dog the

SKC Ch. Elzbieta's Polish Jazz, owned by Donna Gray.

appearance of having faults that do not exist. Although they are independent thinkers, a well-trained PON will easily respond to gentle handling.

Initially, your dog must be taught to walk on both a tight and loose lead. Working with your dog slowly for short periods of time at first will help him to enjoy the routine. Never allow your PON to stop working when he wants. Make sure it is your idea. PONs are smart, and soon they will learn to control you, instead of you controlling them.

The routine of dog showing is going around the ring counterclockwise, and then straight away and return. The second step is a little more difficult because the judge will often want to see the dog move on a loose lead, in order to see the natural movement. It is often difficult for a novice handler to do

this. It is at this time that you will want to show the judge all of the dog's good points, and there is little or no time for corrections. This is the step that takes a lot of practice and patience. Teach your dog to go straight at your left side without pulling.

A PON is usually a good eater, so there is not usually a problem in "baiting" him. Baiting means allowing him to smell and see a small piece of food, enticing him to move any way you want, knowing that shortly he will actually be given this piece of food. Baiting does have its drawbacks, as PONs can get so excited over the smell of food that they sometimes jump, twist, turn, and get out of control trying to reach the food. It is sometimes better to close your hand and pretend there is something in it rather than actually carrying food.

It is necessary to teach your dog

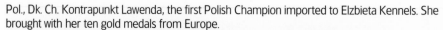

Pol., Dk. Ch. Kontrapunkt Lawenda, the first Polish Champion imported to Elzbieta Kennels. She brought with her ten gold medals from Europe.

BIS Int., Mex., SKC Ch. Drobna z Elzbieta.

to stand still and allow the judge to touch him from head to toe (and testicles if applicable). If you are attending handling classes, let an experienced handler give you advice on how to make this as pleasant an experience as possible for your PON.

The best way to get started in dog showing is to enter your dog in as many fun matches as possible in order for him to learn to be around many other dogs and slowly become comfortable going in the ring. You will then have him relaxed when it is time for his first real show. Fun matches help both the new handler and the dog avoid embarrassment in the real show ring. When your PON is trained to be shown and his coat is in good condition, you can enter him in rare breed shows, States Kennel

Club (SKC) shows, and United Kennel Club (UKC) shows.

It is important that you recognize both the good and bad points about your dog. By grooming, you can minimize its imperfections and maximize its excellent qualities.

In order to show your dog to his best advantage, your own appearance and attire should be taken into consideration. At a dog show, you are not the one in the spotlight. You are the backdrop for your dog, and it is you that must complement him. You should select clothing that is quite comfortable for walking and bending and which will not impede either your own or your dog's movement. You can further enhance your dog's appearance by selecting clothing in a color which offsets or complements the coat

In the ring at the first National Specialty, held in Washington, DC. Judge, Donald Robinder. Photo by T. Borkowski.

SKC Ch. Inbred Lapowka taking Best of Breed at the first National Specialty. Pictured are Enid Bergstrom, editor of Dog World, Cle Francis, editor of the western division of Dog World, the Ambassador of Poland, Margaret Supronowicz, Judge Donald Robinder, and APONC Director John Ford. At this same event, Ms. Bergstrom and Mr. Francis were honored for their recognition of the Pon in *Dog World*.

Dorene Zalis, one of the founders of APONC, with "Cricket" and "Zoe." Dorene died in June 1994. She was the first exhibitor in the US to finish all of her PONs with international championships.

A winning puppy! Shaggy Pons Duzy Bozolski with owner/handler Loana Shields.

color of your dog. You and your dog should present a picture of harmonious movement and color. This will help your dog to look his best.

Bathing, nail trimming, teeth cleaning, and major grooming should be done at home before going to the show. Before you go into the ring, another brushing will be necessary for the final

down, then forward toward the head. Back legs should be brushed forward and then down to show the hocks and proper angulation.

Good ring manners are important. Even though you are mainly paying attention to your dog, remember to look and listen to the judge for requests and directions. Remember not to

PON lovers and their PONs gather together at the first National Specialty.

touches. Remember that the PON's head is supposed to look larger than it actually is. When you brush him, brush the top and the sides of his head to make the head look fuller. If the coat is long, it will part naturally. Do not deliberately part the coat, as it should look as natural as possible. Legs should look as full as possible. First, the hair on the front legs should be brushed

disturb other dogs by standing too close or interfere in any way when the judge is going over another dog. If you are happy with your dog, let him know it when the judge is busy with another dog, but if you are unhappy with him, never correct him in the show ring. In time, your dog will learn to accent his good points and minimize his bad points, both in grooming and showing.

No dog is perfect, but study him well and learn to make the most of him. Work with him at home and have another member of the family gait him, so you can see both front and rear. Notice if he moves better with a loose lead or a tight one. If his topline is not his best point, try not to show it unless it is necessary.

When moving the dog, take him away from the judge and directly back, unless the judge gives you instructions to make a triangle. Should he do so, when returning to him, try to stack your dog on a slight 45-degree angle instead of at a right angle. A quick turn back at this point will cause the coat to fluff and show your dog to its best advantage.

Before the show, have a friend act as a judge. Let him go over and handle the dog so that he is not afraid of strangers. Give him as much exposure as possible to other dogs, people, cars, and unusual situations before the day of the show. It is your job to orient him to unusual circumstances, as he can only perform as well as you have taught him.

Your dog will perform at his best if you are relaxed and enjoying what you are doing. So, enjoy your dog and have a lot of fun with your magnificent companion in the show ring.

SKC Ch. Europa Casimir z Elzbieta CD, by Elzbieta's Pan Vladek ex Ch. Vladja z Elzbieta. Owners, Loana Shields and Tom Wason.

Once aPON a time...Int., So.Am., P.R., SKC Ch. Elzbieta's Drzowie z Rockrun, aka "Zoe," at ten months of age. Owner, Dorene Zalis.

Choosing Your PON Puppy

If you have decided to purchase a purebred dog, you should spend your money wisely. You should expect to receive a healthy animal, having had all the vaccinations and treatment required in his first few weeks of life, medical records attesting to that fact, a written statement guaranteeing the puppy's good health for a limited period of time, and a three or four generation pedigree. You should also be able to see or be informed about both parents of the puppy.

It is not difficult to find a good-quality PON puppy, but it may take time. There are PON breeders in all parts of the U.S. today. To locate a breeder close to you or one with available puppies, contact the PON breed club, APONC, at 1115 Delmont Road, Severn, MD 21144. Once an agreement is reached with a

Pick me! Seven-week-old PON puppies from Elzbieta Kennels. If possible, take the opportunity to observe your prospective pup's interactions with its littermates. Photo by B. Augustowski.

breeder, you may be put on a list and have to wait several months to get your puppy.

It is best if you can pick your puppy personally, and see his littermates and one or both parents, but if that is not possible, you can ask your breeder to pick the best puppy for you and send him to your nearest airport. If this mode is used, the dog must be examined by a veterinarian before flying, and the dog must be transported in a special airline crate. Sometimes a non-stop airline flight can be quicker and less traumatic for a young puppy than a long car ride.

Which is the best puppy for you? Would you prefer a male or a female? Do you want a lively, outgoing, precocious pet or a more sedate companion? How about a show dog and/or a breeder? These are questions

A young PON with breeder/owner Margaret Supronowicz.

Like other breeds of dog, PON puppies spend a good deal of time nestling together and sleeping. These youngsters are a month old. Photo by T. Borkowski.

SKC Ch. Inbred Lapowka nursing her hungry three-day-old litter. The sire of these pups is Pan Vladek.

that must be pondered and discussed with your breeder before settling on the right dog for you.

There is not a significant difference between the temperaments of male and female PONs. Males are generally more active and independent than females and may be a better choice for a child, while mature females, somewhat lazy and more affectionate, could better suit an older person. Unneutered females, of course, have "seasons," a slight incovenience that must be dealt with every six to eight months.

As with children, it is impossible to define a "normal" PON temperament. Temperaments can vary, even in the same litter, but a few generalities can be made. Many PON puppies appear bold and brassy, while some of their littermates seem laid back, even withdrawn. In many other breeds, prospective owners are routinely advised to select the most outgoing puppy to ensure that their dog is not a timid or nervous one. In the PON breed, however, insecurity is never a problem, and the less aggressive puppy will most likely develop into a delightful companion animal, while the more gregarious pup may be a perpetual whirlwind of activity and cheekiness. The behavior of

This PON bitch gave birth the day after this photo was taken. Her belly fur has been clipped to make nursing easier for her puppies. Photo by T. Borkowski.

the puppies should be observed, their reactions to surroundings noted, and their personalities classified as active or passive, independent or socially adaptive, dominant or submissive. It is helpful if a puppy meets his new owner's needs and matches his personality.

If you would like to show and possibly breed your PON, tell your breeder you are interested in a show-quality dog. A dog with show potential should conform closely to the breed standard. A bad bite, a dog too large or too small, a dog with insufficient substance, poor movement are some faults that will penalize a dog in the show ring, but certainly would not bar him from being a perfectly fine pet. If you are paying top dollar for a dog sold as show quality, ask the breeder to explain how the dog is free from major faults and why it is higher priced than others in the litter. There are no hard and fast guarantees as to a puppy's full potential, but if a litter of puppies has been graded by an expert in the breed, your chances of getting what you bargained for are greatly enhanced. Also, the older the puppy is, the easier it is to assess his show quality. When it comes to selling their puppies, many breeders of show dogs will offer contracts with strings attached. If this is the case, be sure you understand all the terms of the contract: whether you are free to neuter if you wish, whether you are expected to show the dog to his championship before breeding, what it means if your breeder is a co-owner of your dog, and so forth.

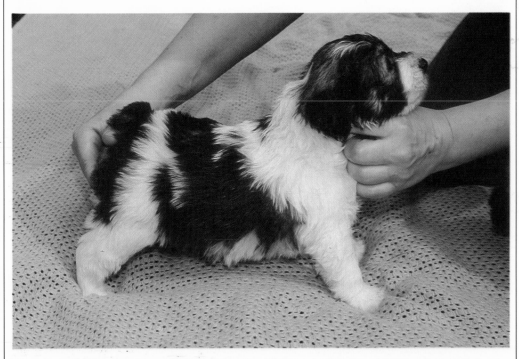

The same male puppy at seven weeks of age (above) and three and one-half months of age (below). Notice the distinct change in the coloration of the coat, a characteristic that is not uncommon in the PON.

These PON puppies are ready to go to their new homes. PON temperament can vary markedly, even among members of the same litter. Photo by Jeannie Kidd.

The PON Puppy

THE NEW ARRIVAL

A puppy can be taken from his mother and littermates as early as seven or eight weeks of age, if someone is available to stay with him most of the time for his first few weeks in his new home. During this period, time must be spent with the puppy observing his behavior, and housetraining and socializing him.

ABOUT CAGES AND CRATES

Very young puppies need a lot of time to sleep and rest, roughly half the hours in a day. It is beneficial if the puppy has his own place where he can rest undisturbed and feel safe and secure. For this purpose, a wire crate is advisable. The #300 crate is a good size for both the young and full-grown PON. Many people have an aversion to putting a dog in a cage; they will feel better if they can be made to see the advantages of giving a den animal a place to call his own. A crate is mobile and can be carried to any room or taken outside the home to afford the dog a familiar haven anywhere you want to take him. He can sleep in your bedroom Crates can be misused, but if young puppies are allowed to enter or exit their crates at will during daytime hours and are never punished in their crates or routinely locked in them for hours on end, crates can be a very

Jande's Sofia PONdering her future. With love and proper care, your PON will thrive and will make a fine family pet. Bred by Janet Masters Campbell.

humane and useful training tool. The puppy can be confined to his crate for short periods for his own safety when he is unattended and at night for as short a period as possible at first. When he has learned to keep clean at night and is over the chewing stage, regular use of the crate can be terminated. A mature dog will usually be perfectly happy to spend time in his crate when the occasion warrants it, such as when traveling or going to dog shows. All PON owners should consider crate training so as to have a safe place to leave a potentially destructive and house-soiling puppy in the owner's absence.

HOME ALONE

It is not advisable to leave a young puppy recently removed from his natural family alone in his new home or backyard. After

PON puppies photographed before tail docking. Some are born with long tails; others are born with very short tails. Photo by T. Borkowski.

leaving the warmth and security of life with his mother and brothers and sisters, a puppy understandably will have moments of unhappiness and loneliness. He needs time to adjust; to leave a young social animal completely alone at this stage is cruel and extremely stressful. As with a young child, it is important to shield your young puppy from as much stress as possible during his early puppyhood.

MANNERS

It is very important before a puppy comes into his new home to establish with all household members exactly what the dog is allowed and forbidden to do, such as: whether or not the puppy is allowed to get up on furniture; if he can be fed from the table during mealtimes; if he can bark when the phone rings or when someone knocks on the door; if he can jump up on people when he is happy to see them; if he is allowed to sleep in a family member's bed, and so on. Bad habits are easily established when PONs are not subject to strict rules. Their memories are phenomenal, and that can either work for you or against you. Also remember that a PON loves to please, but he can't read your mind. Your wishes must be made explicitly clear to him.

FEEDING

Your puppy should be fed at the same time and place every day. He should not be allowed to be hungry or to be overfed. A normal PON puppy, at eight weeks, will eat approximately two to three cups of a good quality puppy food in three or four servings.

HAPPY DAYS

Your PON's waking hours should be spent becoming accustomed to new words and surroundings, slowly and without trauma. The puppy should first be allowed to explore the rooms where he will spend most of his time, experiencing pleasurable activities. He can gradually be acclimated to broader horizons and introduced to new faces. You should try to protect your PON, as much as possible, from situation that are frightening, however some small stresses and surprises are necessary for normal mental development.

It is also important to have lots of physical contact with the puppy. You have to pet and praise him when he does

SKC Ch. Jande Stefan z Europa at five months of age. Family and friends also know him as Stevie Wonder and Stefanski.

something good or is quiet. This is important to do when introducing the puppy to new surroundings and people, especially children.

A happy new mother: Krymka z Kordegardy, the second PON to reside at Elzbieta Kennels, and her litter, sired by Pol. Ch. Apasz z Bankowcow. Krymka gave birth two weeks after her arrival in the US from Poland.

Mother and son: SKC Ch. Elzbieta's Czekolada Shagpon and her son Bozo. PONs are very intelligent dogs, and a good, consistent training program will go a long way in establishing desirable behavior.

Early Training and Socialization

HOUSEBREAKING

As a rule, PONs are not difficult to housebreak, given the opportunity and the time necessary to learn. A new owner must be willing and able to give freely of his time and attention to the puppy for the first few weeks in his new home. The easiest time to housebreak a pup is between eight and ten weeks of age. The training period will take usually one to three weeks. PONs are very easy to housebreak. It is rare that normal, healthy PON puppies will need more than a few lessons. Very often, new owners are surprised that their PONs are so intelligent, the lessons are so short, and the puppy understands so quickly.

Since breeders usually rely on newspapers to help keep litter pens tidy, your new puppy will probably be accustomed to going on newspapers. You can take advantage of this routine by keeping newspapers near the door that you are using to go out with the puppy. When the puppy is

Pol. Ch. Zadymka Koncept keeps watch while two-month-old Hilary snoozes. The PON can be a capable family guard dog. Photo by A. Jedrasiak.

A celebrity Pon: Bobnushka z Elzbieta, better known as "Bob," has appeared in several TV commercials. Owner, John Richardson. Photo by B. Augustowski.

ready to relieve himself, he will start sniffing or turning around on the newspaper and you can speedily take him out. Catching him in the act is essential so that you can praise him lavishly when he does what he is supposed to do outside, and admonish him when he goes inside. Always use the same word to correct him. There is no need to spank him or "rub his nose in it" when he has an accident in the house; your tone of voice and expression will tell him all he needs to know when he has displeased you, and the same is true when you are happy with him.

Walking your puppy as soon as he awakens from a nap and after every meal and before bed at night not only facilitates housebreaking, but is also a quality activity for dog and owner. Be sure to take your puppy out as late as possible at night to shorten the time period when he must keep dry until morning. The puppy should be fed at the same times every day and

also be encouraged to relieve himself immediately afterwards. By your doing this and paying close attention to him during his waking hours, catching him sniffing or circling on the newspapers and rushing him outdoors, he will soon adjust to the habit of urinating and defecating outside.

SMART DOGS

PONs are very clever dogs, and it is nearly impossible to find one that is difficult to train. Spending a lot of quality time with your new puppy will pay you rich dividends for a long time to come. PONs love to be obedient; they love to do what we want them to do and they do it happily and quickly. PONs can understand much more than we expect them to, and it is rare for an owner who is teaching his PON from the beginning to experience any behavior problems.

BONDING

The initial time that you spend training your PON will not only teach him how to be a socially acceptable member of your household, but it will also speed and reinforce the bonding process between you and him. Close interaction with his new master will instill in him feelings of confidence and trust, which will enable him to cope with all the new experiences awaiting him.

FOLLOW THE LEADER

Pet/owner bonding is critical to a well-balanced dog's development. Perhaps the easiest bonding process is a simple follow-the-leader exercise. Place the puppy on the ground and slowly walk away from him calling his name, gesturing for him to follow you. Usually the puppy will follow you, and when he does, he should be praised and petted so that he knows he is doing something good. This is his first lesson in learning how to be obedient. Everyone in the family should do the same exercise during the puppy's first few weeks in his new home, to accustom him to follow those whom he knows. Housebreaking and training to follow should be started as soon as the puppy is brought home.

TO CHEW OR NOT TO CHEW

It is also important to teach the puppy very early not to chew on things not meant to be chewed, such as your belongings and the hands of those playing with the puppy. The dog should have a plethora of safe chew toys, such as those made by Nylabone, to play with. Teaching your dog to retrieve a ball or rubber toy and return it to you is enjoyable for both participants.

THE BACKYARD BARKER

Some owners will find that a PON, who loves to be with people, will hate to stay at home or outside in the backyard by himself. In such situations, you have to realize that he will use all his cleverness to get out of a situation where he finds himself alone. A PON left outside by himself may bark and bark incessantly. He must be

disciplined from the beginning not to do this. Try leaving him for very short periods while he is young, praising him on your return when he is quiet. It is not difficult to train a PON to be a perfectly behaved pet. We should remember that training and teaching is a long process. If a PON is allowed to behave badly, he will remember that he was allowed to misbehave, and he will continue to do so.

HAPPY HEELING

During quiet play periods, leash training can be started. Leash training should commence when the puppy is three to four months of age. Walking on the leash is not a PON's favorite activity. A PON would much rather follow his

Przemek's Latka and pal Heather. A PON needs to spend quality time with members of his human family. Photo by T. Borkowski.

All in a PON's day's work...Klon Akribeia tending a wayward lamb at Elzbieta Kennels.

leader wherever he goes, with his nose nearly touching his master's leg. Many PON owners only use the leash in training and permit their dog to walk freely in safe environments. If your PON is very obedient, always coming to you when called, allow him to walk off the leash as much as possible when there is no danger of traffic or other loose animals.

SCHOOL DAYS

If puppy training classes are available, the puppy and his owner should be enrolled when the PON is three to four months old. Attending puppy kindergarten is the best way to socialize a young dog and introduce him to other dogs and friendly people. The owner will see the capabilities of his dog and will be less likely to make excuses for his pet's misbehavior. Remember, a PON loves to please, so you will find this breed very amenable to obedience training.

TRICKS OF THE TRADE

Teaching the dog how to sit, lie down, roll over, and give his paw can be practical, useful training to quiet an anxious animal or to stop one from jumping up on people when he is excited. It is much easier to control a dog if "sit" and "down" commands are well understood. PONs love to do tricks, and it is not hard to teach them. The only things needed are your good ideas and consistency in teaching them. This training is most successful if conducted when your PON is four to six months of age.

YOUNG AT HEART

PONs generally mature, mentally and physically, early. A one-year-old PON is nearly fully developed, although he will often act like a puppy. He will retain many of the habits and behaviors he exhibited as a pup for a very long time. A PON can be a serious and diligent worker and then, at playtime, be as frolicsome as a pup.

Nutrition for the PON

As experienced and non-experienced dog owners know, a proper diet is very important in keeping a dog healthy and in good condition. Dogs need a quality diet carefully formulated to ensure digestibility, as well as availability of essential amino acids, minerals, vitamins, and essential fatty acids for the maintenance of good skin and coat condition. The proper fiber level is also important for good digestive functions.

All dogs are not the same; feeding requirements differ according to physiological status, health, age, temperament, and many other variables. The nutritional needs of a working Siberian Husky cannot be compared with those of an Italian Greyhound, nor should the diet of an active PON with farm duties be the same as that fed to a couch potato PON. In addition to tailoring a dog's diet to his individual needs and requirements, some breeds, such as the PON, require specific diets for optimum quality of life.

Choosing the correct commercial dog food can be a difficult problem for a concerned dog owner trying to find the best diet for his pet. Most of today's pet foods have taste appeal, colors and shapes that are

Normally, a PON puppy at the age of eight weeks will eat about two to three cups of a good quality puppy food in three or four daily servings. Photo by T. Borkowski.

attractive to the buyer. The pet food industry, approaching sales of several billion dollars a year, offers hundreds of types of diets, conveniently packaged and readily available. Manufacturers of pet foods are quick to sense and respond to trendy consumer concerns, offering, for instance, "lite" pet foods, pet foods low in fat and salt, "all natural" pet foods, even pet foods with "garden vegetables." Many of the health concerns of humans are not applicable to dogs, thus making most pet "health foods" unnecessary and a waste of money. Most pet owners make decisions on pet food based on price and advertisement, and not on the needs of their pet.

The Polski Owczarek Nizinny, an old herding breed indigenous to the lowlands of Central Europe, has aided Polish farmers and shepherds for centuries. All dogs are carnivorous, and the PON is no exception, but these dogs rarely had the chance to eat meat and bones. So what did the hardy herders subsist on during Poland's turbulent past? The PON diet, even in modern-day Poland, consists of bread, potatoes, small amounts of cottage cheese, milk, and an occasional egg. Also, it is well known that the natural supplement of vitamins and minerals was obtained from eating the feces of grass-eating animals. PONs have always been known as very hardworking dogs that thrived on a limited diet. Excellent eaters, PONs will normally accept almost everything that is edible, devour it like a

vacuum, and be ready for another offer of food immediately thereafter.

Since the PON became a household pet, two major problems have been observed: obesity and itchiness with no primary skin problems. Overweight dogs become less active and, as a result, their nutritional requirements change. A less active PON should not consume the same amount of calories as an active one, but he still needs good natural food to maintain muscle, skin and coat condition, as well as other bodily functions.

Due to the feeding history of generations of PONs, it is believed that the PON's metabolism has adjusted to low-protein food. Although the simple foods offered to working PONs since the 19th century on Polish farms may seem insufficient to us, the diet contained enough quality protein to keep the dogs hardy, healthy, and useful. Three factors determine protein quality: completeness of digestion, absorption, and utilization.

The significant term in feeding protein is its "biological value." The higher the biological value rating, the more useful the protein is to the dog. Egg, meat meal, and cottage cheese are on the top of the list, while wheat, corn, and gluten feed are far lower. PONs need less overall "energy foods" then we expect, small amounts of protein with good biological value, proper fiber level, vitamins, and minerals.

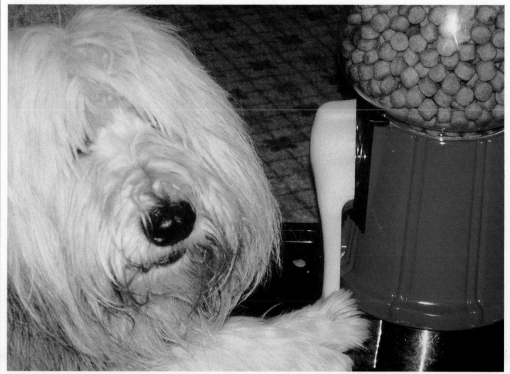

PONs have hearty appetites. Here's "Oliver" (Elzbieta's Oliver Zingle) helping himself to some chow. Owner, Katy Zingle.

PUPPY CHOW

Dog breeders routinely give their puppies food that is rich in protein, calcium, and easily digested carbohydrates. People new to the science of dog breeding may not realize that excess levels of nutrients and calories are just as harmful as insufficient levels. Some commercial pet foods have more nutrients than are necessary to protect against deficiency. This is counterproductive. Recent studies on nutritionally induced disease problems in dogs have revealed that too much of certain nutrients such as calcium, iodine, and vitamins A and D can result in nutritional diseases. There have been several reports of dermatology problems in dogs that have been responsive to additional dietary zinc. These nutritional abnormalities can cause severe, or even fatal, clinical problems in animals.

In Poland, PON puppies are fed cottage cheese, egg yolks, fresh vegetables, fresh meat, and some carbohydrates, such as spaghetti, rice, and bread. It has been observed that when feeding PON puppies a very high-protein diet, they would scratch themselves for no apparent reason. The same syndrome was observed in adult PONs. Experienced PON breeders in America have found that a protein-rich diet given "ad libitum" (with no limit) causes itching in their dogs. This

Elzbieta's Malgosia getting into mischief. It is important that you establish "house rules" while your PON is still a puppy. Photo by T. Borkowski.

behavior understandably distresses owners. They call their veterinarian for help and are usually faced with extensive diagnostic procedures and unsuccessful therapy. As a last resort, the veterinarian may prescribe cortisone to treat the itching, which will cause an increase in appetite. Thus, skin problems and obesity in PONs could be a simple result of the improper feeding of commercial dog food. Weight problems are a result of too little activity, too many calories, or both. Itching is frequently a nutritionally induced disease in terms of excessive levels of certain nutrients.

Experience has shown that the natural foods used to feed PONs in Poland in past and present times are nutritionally complete and balanced for puppies and dogs.

Your PON's diet should be nutritionally balanced to ensure optimum development. Excess—or insufficient—levels of various nutrients can lead to problems such as itching.

Your Aging PON

Aging is a normal part of life and has to be understood and appreciated as any other season of your dog's life. PONs are known to have a longer life span than many giant breeds but do not live as long as some toy breeds. In Poland, PONs are considered old at about seven or eight years of age and are really old at 10 to 12 years of age. They have generally been found to have a much longer life span here in the U.S.

PONs usually advance into old age without major changes in their health. They become less active and energetic, need more sleep, and become less involved in the world around them. Alertness, speed, and interest in previous activities decline. They become less tolerant as their entire world gets smaller, and they need comfort, support, and love.

Your aging dog is facing many discomforts. His senses are failing, and this can change his behavior. Before correcting him, you should carefully consider the particular situation. You must realize that your older dog requires more sleep. He needs more frequent, but smaller, meals of higher biological value, containing less minerals. He needs more frequent trips to relieve himself. His metabolism is slowing down, but you should maintain his condition so that he is neither too thin nor obese.

PONs are never poor eaters, and this can be a problem. It is essential that your PON not eat too much or become overweight, which could significantly shorten his activity and life span. It is important to maintain an ideal weight with low calorie intake and balanced nutrition. This means a formula that is low in fat and high in dietary fiber. Increased fiber helps your dog feel less hungry and decreases and helps regulate moisture content of the feces to aid normal bowel movement. Older PONs need a lower quantity of protein with higher nutritional value.

Diets that are lower in protein also assist in maintaining normal kidney function. It is well known that many dogs in their middle years have kidney dysfunctions. Lower amounts of minerals can help to reduce the effects of kidney dysfunction.

As your PON ages, his teeth, heart, lungs, eyes, and ears may also begin to show signs of slow and gradual deterioration. Regular annual visits to your vet become even more important at this time. Resistance to disease decreases as your PON ages. Dental plaque formation will result in gum disease and loss of teeth, accompanied by bad breath. Gum disease is more

PON pups are indeed a handful! Laura Gardzelewski with PON littermates bred by Roy and Kim Richmond.

tumors under the skin, eye diseases, cataracts and blindness, and stiff joints causing lameness.

Older dogs like to sleep a lot, and after waking up they are often stiff and slow moving. Exercise your older PON, but in moderation. Your pet tires more easily now. It is beneficial for the dog to take shorter, but more frequent, walks. Your older dog should not be exposed to extremely hot or cold temperatures.

Regular bathing is very important for the older dog, and it gives you a chance to examine your PON carefully from head to toe. Your dog's skin and coat can tell you a lot about his health. Any tumors, pain, inflammation, or signs of irritation should be brought to the attention of your veterinarian.

Older dogs need a regular daily routine. Keep this routine stable. Don't give your dog any surprises. Never leave him alone in strange environments.

Careful, regular observation of your PON as he gradually ages is very important. You have to be aware of any little changes and detect signs of trouble in order to ensure that he gets the medical attention he needs. You have to be very patient. Most PONs age without personality changes. A few become more stubborn or difficult. You have to be prepared to love your beloved companion until the very end, because he needs you and you are his best friend.

common than most dog owners think. It is estimated that 85 to 90 percent of dogs over three to four years of age have some degree of gum disease. Common signs of teeth and gum problems are: bad breath, irritated gums with tartar deposits, less activity than usual, excessive salivation, pain in the mouth, reluctance to eat, and blood in the saliva.

Other frequent signs of illness are hearing loss, uncontrolled urination, increased water intake or frequent urination, lumps or

The PON in Poland and Europe

DOG HISTORY IN POLAND

Interest in dog breeding has been traditional in Poland for centuries. The following is a brief listing of some of the many noteworthy events in the history of the dog in Poland:

1112—The first remarks concerning dogs were recorded in *Chronicles* by Gail Anomimus.

1387—The Polish King Wladyslaw Jaqirallo was a great enthusiast of dogs and hunting. He established a higher penalty for stealing a dog than for killing a man.

1590—The sight hounds were mentioned for the first time in a book written by Jan Ostrorog, entitled *Hunting With Hounds.*

1779—Kluk wrote, "Truly, the best publications about dogs are the English ones, for it is the English who have the greatest skill in the care and management of dogs."

Int., Wd., Pol. Ch. Radosz z Psiego Raju taking BIS at Poznan. Judge, Lucienn Jasica of Belgium. Handler, Eva Adamska. Also pictured are Edmund Defraiteur, Secretary of the FCI, and Marian Szymandera, President of the Poznan Kennel Club.

1823—Several articles about hunting dogs and sighthounds were printed in the journal *Sylwan*. The author described Italian, Egyptian, Scottish, and Polish sighthounds. He gave a detailed description of the Polish Sighthounds.

1881—The first dog show known in the history of the Polish Kennel Club was organized in Warsaw.

1889—The show of hunting dogs and sighthounds took place at 35 Nowy Swiat Street in Warsaw. The Polish Kennel Club maintains its headquarters at this address to this day.

1924—An organization of breeders of purebred dogs was formed in Warsaw. Before 1924, breed clubs were independent all over Poland.

1925—The stud book registry started in Warsaw. The

International marriage: SKC Ch. Inbred Lapowka with her "husband" from Poland, Pol. Ch. Premier Oligarchia. Photo by T. Borkowski.

first national dog show took place in Warsaw.

1938—The Polish Kennel Club was established before World War II and was accepted by the FCI. The war brought everything to a complete standstill.

1945—After the war, the Hunters Association took care of hunting dogs, and working and sporting dog clubs began again in other parts of Poland.

1948—An organizational meeting of breeds took place on May 5.

1948—The Polish Kennel Club was re-established with its main office in Warsaw. The other district clubs became branches of the Polish Kennel Club.

1957—The Polish Kennel Club became a member of the FCI.

1968—Mr. Edward Milulaki of Poland was elected President of the FCI.

Before coming to the US, Lapowka won a Junior Winner title and Polish Kennel Club Certificate of Merit in Poland. Photo by T. Borkowski.

PON NATIONAL SPECIALTY SHOWS IN POLAND
During the National Specialty Show, an international meeting and symposium are held. All subjects connected with the breed are discussed, and observations about breed development are presented. The National Specialty for the years 1975, 1978, 1984, 1988, and 1990 were held in Bydgoszcz, Poland.

Year	Number of Dogs Entered	Best Male	Best Female
1975	72	Gwarek z Psiego Raju	Cuma Spod Zagla
1978	91	Limbo Urania	Czajka z Zeriby
1984	135	Apasz Bankowcow	Arkonia z Kordegardy
1988		Palasz z Wielgowa	Arkonia z Kordegardy
1990	96	Bartnik z Matecznika Diany	Fryga Moscic

Pol. Ch. Kalina Rawipon, by Ch. Apasz z Bankowcow ex Jemiola z Kordegardy, at one year of age. Shown with Agata Kowalyk. The PON's popularity has risen steadily since its reemergence after the end of World War II.

PON WORLD CHAMPIONS FROM POLAND

During the "Iron Curtain" era, it was extremely difficult for Polish people to go abroad with their dogs. To become an International Champion, a dog has to win four international shows in three different countries that are members of the FCI. During this time, East Germany, the Soviet Union, and Romania were not FCI members.

Dog's Name	Where and When Title Was Acquired
Lancet z Zeriby	Dortmund, Germany 1981
Malwina z Kordegardy	Madrid, Spain 1983
Arkonia z Kordegardy	Copenhagen, Denmark 1989
Radosz z Psiego Raju	Copenhagen, Denmark 1989
Ruslan Loza	Brno, Czechoslovakia 1990
Bartnik z Matecznika Diany	Dortmund, Germany 1991

Above: Pol. Ch. Sultan Pacynka. **Bottom**: Ch. Kaszanka von Goralenhoff, a black and tan PON.

INTERNATIONAL CHAMPIONS (LIVING IN POLAND)

Dog's Name	Year of Championship
Amok Moniek	1969
(First International PON Champion)	
Gazda z Psiego Raju	1977
Forga z Kordegardy	1978
Doman z Kordegardy	1979
Jonat z Zeriby	1980
Zazula z Psiego Raju	1981
Malwina z Kordegardy	1984
Oda Brzozka z Psiego Raju	1986
Radosz z Psiego Raju	1990
Arkonia z Kordegardy	1990
Czekan Moscic	1990
Duga Jaga z Kordegardy	1990

Kontrapunkt Jaka Taka, by Kontrapunkt Ulan ex Lubianka z Kordegardy. Photo by J. Staniszewska.

MOST-TITLED AND BEST-KNOWN PONS IN EUROPE

AGUSIA Z NADWARCIANSKIEJ DOLINY—Polish, Czechoslovakian, and International Champion

Date of Birth: March 15, 1975
Sire: Matros z Kordegardy
Dam: Domka z Psiego Raju

AKIS V. PON-GARTEN—Polish, Danish, Czechoslovakian, Hungarian, and International Champion

Date of Birth: November 10, 1969
Sire: Doman z Kordegardy
Dam: Czeremcha z Kolchidy

ALEGORIA AGIPONIK—Polish Champion

Date of Birth: July 20, 1975
Sire: Matros z Kordegardy
Dam: Jodla z Kordegardy

AMOK MONIEK—Polish and International Champion

Date of Birth: April 27, 1961
Sire: Inkluz z Kordegardy
Dam: Harfa z Kordegardy

ANTEK Z KORDEGARDY—International and Danish Champion

Date of Birth: March 16, 1969
Sire: Doman z Kordegardy
Dam: Beza z Lagiewnickiego Boru

ASCHA LOSH—Belgian, Czechoslovakian, and International Champion

Date of Birth: October 10, 1976
Sire: Zuk-Urania
Dam: Zytnia v.h.Goralenhof

ATA-BIALKA Z KOLCHIDY—Polish Champion

Date of Birth: September 6, 1965
Sire: Inkluz z Kordegardy
Dam: Finka Buba z Psiego Raju

ARKONIA Z KORDEGARDY—
International and Polish
Champion and 1989 World
Champion
  Date of Birth: February 24,
1983
  Sire: Hermes spod Zagla
  Dam: Malwina z Kordegardy
BAJ Z LAGIEWNICKIEGO
BORU—Polish Champion
  Date of Birth: September 1,
1965
  Sire: Amok Moniek
  Dam: Szelma z Kordegardy
BEKS CARIOKA—Polish
Champion
  Date of Birth: June 6, 1970
  Sire: Amok Moniek
  Dam: Ada Krecia z Kolchidy
BIG BURSZTYN Z
KOLCHIDY—Polish Champion
  Date of Birth: July 23, 1966
  Sire: Amok Moniek
  Dam: Finka-Buba z Psiego
Raju
BRONIA ALBINA—
International Champion
  Date of Birth: October 3, 1977
  Sire: Bom ze Zrodel
Solankowych
  Dam: Zaska v.Goralenhof
CEZAR Z HENRYKOWA—
Polish, French, and 1989
Reserve World Champion;
Hungarian Winner
  Date of Birth: December 4,
1982
  Sire: Rumcays z Jurty
  Dam: Lowna z Henrykowa
CUMA SPOD ZAGLA—Polish
Champion
  Date of Birth: December 30,
1966
  Sire: Szkrab z Kordegardy
  Dam: Garda-Wtora z
Kordegardy

Pol. Ch. Cezar z Henrykowa, by Rumcays z Jurty ex Lowna z Henrykowa. Cezar was a Europa 1991 winner.

DANY V. PON-GARTEN—
Czechoslovakian and Danish
Champion
  Date of Birth: January 3, 1974
  Sire: Akis v. Pon-Garten
  Dam: Zofka z Kordegardy
DOMAN Z KORDEGARDY—
Polish, Czechoslovakian, and
International Champion
  Date of Birth: March 9, 1967
  Sire: Lider z Kordegardy
  Dam: Certa z Melna
DOMKA Z KORDEGARDY—
Polish Champion
  Date of Birth: July 13, 1962
  Sire: Inkluz z Kordegardy
  Dam: Kuma z Kordegardy
DOMKA Z PSIEGO RAJU—
Polish Champion
  Date of Birth: February 17,
1973
  Sire: Witez z Kordegardy
  Dam: Rzepicha z Psiego Raju
DRAN Z ZERIBY—Polish
Champion

Date of Birth:
August 8, 1975
Sire: Matros z
Kordegardy
Dam: Lima
Urania
EICKO V. PON-
GARTEN—
Czechoslovakian,
Romanian, and
Hungarian
Champion
Date of Birth:
December 4, 1974
Sire: Akis v. Pon-
Garten

Gaja z Starego Lupkowa, Pol., Dk. Ch. Wacpan z Kordegardy, and Marzanna z Kordegardy. Photo by T. Borkowski.

Dam: Ciana v. Pon-Garten
ELKA SPOD ZAGLA—Polish
Champicn
Date of Birth: November 3,
1969
Sire: Doman z Kordegardy
Dam: Cuma spod Zagla
GARDA SPOD ZAGLA—Polish
Champion
Date of Birth: November 24,
1973
Sire: Akis v. Pon-Garten

Dam: Cuma spod Zagla
GARDA WTORA Z
KORDEGARDY—Polish
Champion
Date of Birth: April 27, 1960
Sire: Asan z Kordegardy
Dam: Kuma z Kordegardy
GAZDA Z PSIEGO RAJU—
Swedish Champion
Date of Birth: September 12,
1973
Sire: Witez z Kordegardy

Enjoying the Polish countryside. Kontrapunkt Furtjanka, Ch. Kontrapunkt Lawenda, Kontrapunkt Jaka Taka, Ch. Tymianka z Amieliowki, and Kontrapunkt Escorta. Photo by J. Staniszewska.

Pol. Ch. Premier Oligarchia, by Kusy Kawalkada ex Wena Pacynka-Oligarchia. Photo by T. Borkowski.

Dam: Rzepicha z Psiego Raju
GROG SPOD ZAGLA—Polish Champion
Date of Birth: November 24, 1973
Sire: Akis v. Pon-Garten
Dam: Cuma spod Zagla
GROM Z KORDEGARDY—Polish Champion
Date of Birth: September 15, 1969
Sire: Doman z Kordegardy
Dam: Hajda z Kordegardy
GROZA Z ZORIBY—Polish Champion
Date of Birth: April 2, 1977
Sire: Jurand z Grenady
Dam: Lima Urania
GWAREK Z PSIEGO RAJU—Polish Champion
Date of Birth: September 12, 1973
Sire: Witez z Kordegardy
Dam: Rzepicha z Psiego Raju
GWARKA KERBERAC'S

HOLANDIA—Dutch Champion
Date of Birth: February 8, 1976
Sire: Ascar of the White Voliant
Dam: Vania v. Goralenhof
IGOR Z ZERIBY—Polish Champion
Date of Birth: March 10, 1979
Sire: Jurand z Grenady
Dam: Lima Urania
JODLA Z KORDEGARDY—Polish and Czechoslovakian Champion
Date of Birth: January 29, 1972
Sire: Doman z Kordegardy
Dam: Lonka z Kordegardy
JONATAN Z ZERIBY—Polish and International Champion
Date of Birth: July 8, 1975
Sire: Matros z Kordegardy
Dam: Zenia Urania
KUBA Z OGRODKA MAGDY—Czechoslovakian Champion

Laszka z Kordegardy, by Ch. Apasz z Bankowcow ex Plaza z Kordegardy. Shown with Agata Kowalyk.

Date of Birth: September 6, 1978
   Sire: Cis spod Winnego Krzewu
   Dam: Agusia z Nadwarcianskiej Doliny
   LADA Z KORDEGARDY—Polish Champion
   Date of Birth: March 30, 1972
   Sire: Doman z Kordegardy
   Dam: Kuma z Kordegardy
   LANCET Z ZERIBY—Polish Champion
   Date of Birth: November 6,

Champion
   Date of Birth: April 15, 1972
   Sire: Grom z Kordegardy
   Dam: Witra Urania
   LUNA Z KORDEGARDY—Swedish Champion
   Date of Birth: January 14, 1974
   Sire: Zyndram z Kordegardy
   Dam: Lada z Kordegardy
   MALWINA Z KORDEGARDY—Polish, Czechoslovakian, and International Champion; World

Pol., Dk. Ch. Kontrapunkt Lawenda. One of Lawenda's many attributes was her gentle disposition.

1977
   Sire: Jurand z Grenady
   Dam: Oda Urania
   LEON KERBERAC'S HOLANDIA—Dutch Champion
   Date of Birth: April 4, 1978
   Sire: Zywy v. Goralenhof
   Dam: Gwarka Kerberac's Holandia
   LIMBO URANIA—Polish

Champion, Madrid 1983
   Date of Birth: July 12, 1978
   Sire: Kompan z Kordegardy
   Dam: Drumla z Kordegardy
   MATROS Z KORDEGARDY—Polish Champion
   Date of Birth: May 29, 1972
   Sire: Grzmot z Kordegardy
   Dam: Elegia z Kordegardy
   MUFKA Z KORDEGARDY—

Pol. Ch. Turon z Psiego Raju, by Gwarek z Psiego Raju ex Olga z Psiego Raju. Turon is the sire of Pan Vladek, the foundation dog at Elzbieta Kennels. Photo by T. Borkowski.

Polish Champion
Date of Birth: July 14, 1970
Sire: Doman z Kordegardy
Dam: Beza z Lagiewnickiego Boru
MUSZLA Z KORDEGARDY—
Dutch Champion
Date of Birth: May 29, 1972
Sire: Grzmot z Kordegardy
Dam: Elegia z Kordegardy
PAJDA Z KORDEGARDY—
Polish Champion
Date of Birth: September 9, 1978
Sire: Grog spod Zagla
Dam: Ustka z Kordegardy
PING-CZIN Z KORDEGARDY—
Polish Champion
Date of Birth: April 24, 1966
Sire: Inkluz z Kordegardy
Dam: Certa z Melna
POLON Z KORDEGARDY—
Polish Champion

Date of Birth: September 25, 1970
Sire: Doman z Kordegardy
Dam: Isia z Kordegardy
RADOSZ Z PSIEGO RAJU—
Polish, International, and World Champion, 1990
Date of Birth: July 7, 1983
Sire: Gwarek z Psiego Raju
Dam: Bella z Nadwarcianskiej Doliny
RETMAN Z PSIEGO RAJU—
Danish, Czechoslovakian, and International Champion
Date of Birth: May 3, 1976
Sire: Gwarek z Psiego Raju
Dam: Witra Urania
ROLA Z KORDEGARDY—
Polish and Czechoslovakian Champion
Date of Birth: July 12, 1968
Sire: Lubek z Kordegardy
Dam: Isia z Kordegardy

SUNIA Z KORDEGARDY—
Polish Champion
  Date of Birth: September 2,
1964
  Sire: Inkluz z Kordegardy
  Dam: Isia z Kordegardy
SZELMA Z KORDEGARDY—
Polish Champion
  Date of Birth: May 17, 1963
  Sire: Inkluz z Kordegardy
  Dam: Erga z Babiej Wsi
SZERSZEN Z
KORDEGARDY—Polish
Champion
  Date of Birth: May 17, 1963
  Sire: Inkluz z Kordegardy
  Dam: Erga z Babiej Wsi
TURON Z PSIEGO RAJU—
Polish Champion
  Date of Birth: July 8, 1976
  Sire: Gwarek z Psiego Raju
  Dam: Olga z Psiego Raju
USTKA Z KORDEGARDY—
Polish Champion
  Date of Birth: December 19,

Pol. Ch. Tymianka z Amieliowki, a two-time Reserve World Champion.

1977
  Sire: Doman z Kordegardy
  Dam: Dumka z Kordegardy
VANIA V.
GORALENHOF—Dutch and
International Champion
  Date of Birth: January
24, 1972
  Sire: Zuk Urania
  Dam: Miedza z
Kordegardy
VASCO V.
GORALENHOF—Belgian
Champion
  Date of Birth: January
24, 1972
  Sire: Zuk Urania
  Dam: Miedza z
Kordegardy
WACPAN Z
KORDEGARDY—Polish
Champion
  Date of Birth: March 7,
1979

Pol. Ch. Apasz z Bankowcow in the alert stance typical of the PON. Apasz's name can be found in the pedigrees of many top-winning dogs.

Sire: Dran z Zeriby
Dam: Ustka z Kordegardy
WIGOR-GOL Z JURTY—Polish Champion
Date of Birth: February 26, 1971
Sire: Doman z Kordegardy
Dam: Rola z Kordegardy
WITEZ Z KORDEGARDY—Polish Champion
Date of Birth: September 16, 1968
Sire: Lubek z Kordegardy
Dam: Duda z Kordegardy
XALNY V. GORALENHOF—Dutch and International Champion
Date of Birth: February 21, 1973
Sire: Zuk Urania
Dam: Miedza z Kordegardy
ZAZULA Z PSIEGO RAJU—Dutch and International Champion
Date of Birth: June 10, 1977
Sire: Gwarek z Psiego Raju

Pol. Ch. Zur z Wielgowa, by Olek v.d. Widdenburg ex Ganska Sagittarius.

Dam: Witra Urania
ZMORKA Z PSIEGO RAJU—Polish Champion
Date of Birth: April 11, 1971
Sire: Wiarus z Kordegardy
Dam: Rzepicha z Psiego Raju
ZOFKA Z KORDEGARDY—Danish Champion
Date of Birth: March 8, 1969
Sire: Lubek z Kordegardy
Dam: Hajda z Kordegardy
ZUK URANIA—International Champion
Date of Birth: December 26, 1969
Sire: Cwik spod Zagla
Dam: Arabella z Alty
ZUPAN Z KORDEGARDY—Polish, Danish, and International Champion
Date of Birth: April 14, 1979
Sire: Rumcajs z Jurty
Dam: Lada z Kordegardy
ZWICKLY V. KIMSTANHOERE—Dutch Champion
Date of Birth: April 20, 1979
Sire: Dar z Nadwarcianskiej Doliny
Dam: Axandra v. Menlenhof

BIS, Int., Wd., Pol. Ch. Radosz z Psiego Raju with breeder/owner Tadeusz Adamski. Photo by W. Piatek.

Pol. Ch. Viwat Pacynka proudly displaying his nice head. Viwat, by Ch. Supel Filipon ex Ch. Kalina Rawipon, is a four-time CACIB winner. Photo by J. Zych.

POLISH CHAMPIONS FROM THE BEGINNING UP TO 1990

CHAMPION	DATE OF BIRTH	SIRE	DAM
Garda Wtora z Kordegardy	4-27-60	Asan z Kordegardy	Kuma z Kordegardy
Amok Moniek	4-27-61	Inkluz z Kordegardy	Harfa z Kordegardy
Domka z Kordegardy	7-13-62	Inkluz z Kordegardy	Kuma z Kordegardy
Szelma z Kordegardy	5-17-63	Inkluz z Kordegardy	Erga z Babiej Wsi
Szerszen z Kordegardy			
Lubek z Kordegardy	4-15-64	Arak Greps z Kordegardy	Iwa z Kordegardy
Sunia z Kordegardy	9-2-64	Inkluz z Kordegardy	Isia z Kordegardy
Baj z Lagiewnickiego Boru	9-1-65	Amok Moniek	Szelma z Kordegardy
Ata Bialka z Kordegardy	11-6-65	Inkluz z Kordegardy	Finka Buba z Psiego Raju
Ping Czin z Kordegardy	4-24-66	Inkluz z Kordegardy	Certa z Melna
Big Bursztyn z Kolchidy	7-23-66	Amok Moniek	Finka Buba z Psiego Raju
Cuma spod Zagla	12-30-66	Skrab z Kordegardy	Garda Wtora z Kordegardy
Doman z Kordegardy	3-9-67	Lider z Kordegardy	Certa z Melna
Rola z Kordegardy	7-12-68	Lubek z Kordegardy	Isia z Kordegardy
Witez z Kordegardy	9-16-68	Lubek z Kordegardy	Duda z Kordegardy
Grom z Kordegardy	9-15-69	Doman z Kordegardy	Hajda z Kordegardy
Elka spod Zagla	11-03-69	Doman z Kordegardy	Cuma spod Zagla
Akis v. Pon-Garten	11-10-69	Doman z Kordegardy	Czeremcha z Kordegardy
Beks Carioka	5-6-70	Amok Moniek	Ada Krecia z Kordegardy
Mufka z Kordegardy	7-14-70	Doman z Kordegardy	Beza z Lagiewnickiego Boru
Polon z Kordegardy	9-25-70	Doman z Kordegardy	Isia z Kordegardy
Wigor Gol z Jurty	2-26-71	Doman z Kordegardy	Rola z Kordegardy
Zmorka z Psiego Raju	4-11-71	Wiarus z Kordegardy	Rzepicha z Psiego Raju
Jodla z Kordegardy	1-29-72	Doman z Kordegardy	Lonka z Kordegardy
Lada z Kordegardy	3-30-72	Doman z Kordegardy	Kuma z Kordegardy
Limbo Urania	4-15-72	Grom z Kordegardy	Witra Urania
Matros z Kordegardy	5-29-72	Grzmot z Kordegardy	Elegia z Kordegardy
Domka z Psiego Raju	2-17-73	Witez z Kordegardy	Rzepicha z Psiego Raju
Gwarek z Psiego Raju	9-12-73	Witez z Kordegardy	Rzepicha z Psiego Raju
Garda spod Zagla	11-24-73	Akis v. Pon-Garten	Cuma spod Zagla
Grog spod Zagla	11-24-73	Akis v. Pon-Garten	Cuma spod Zagla
Agusia Nadwarcianska	3-15-75	Matros z Kordegardy	Dolina Domka z Psiego Raju
Jonatan z Zeriby	7-8-75	Matros z Kordegardy	Zenia Urania
Agat Agiponik	7-20-75	Matros z Kordegardy	Jodia z Kordegardy
Alegoria Agiponik	7-20-75	Matros z Kordegardy	Jodia z Kordegardy
Dran z Zeriby	8-8-75	Matros z Kordegardy	Lima Urania
Cis spod Winnego Krzewu	3-12-76	Rubin z Jurty	Watra Wawa Urania
Turon z Psiego Raju	7-8-76	Gwarek z Psiego Raju	Olga z Psiego Raju
Retman z Psiego Raju	5-3-76	Gwartek z Psiego Raju	Witra Urania
Figlarz z Zeriby	8-31-76	Jurand z Grenady	Oda Urania
Groza z Zeriby	4-20-77	Jurand z Grenady	Lima Urania

Lancet z Zeriby	11-6-77	Jurand z Grenady	Oda Urania
Ustka z Korde gardy	2-19-77	Doman z Kordegardy	Dumka z Kordegardy
Malwina z Kordegardy	7-12-78	Kompan z Kordegardy	Drumla z Kordegardy
Kaduk z Ogrodka Magdy	9-6-78	Cis spod Winnego Krzewu	Agusia z Nadw. Doliny
Pajda z Kordegardy	9-9-78	Grog spod Zagla	Ustka z Kordegardy
Wacpan z Kordegardy	3-7-79	Dran z Zeriby	Ustka z Kordegardy
Igor z Zeriby	3-10-79	Jurand z Grenady	Lima Urania
Zupan z Kordegardy	4-14-79	Rumcajs z Jurty	Lada z Kordegardy
Zywia z Kordegardy	4-14-79	Rumcajs z Jurty	Lada z Kordegardy
Apasz z Bankowcow	12-17-79	Jurand z Grenady	Tama Delicja
Szerszen z Zeriby	4-20-80	Jurand z Grenady	Barka z Zeriby
Mrzonka z Kordegardy	11-7-80	Kaduk Tytus	Pajda z Kordegardy
Hadja v.d. Widderburg	12-20-80	Elren v.d. Ponte Nova	Bamby v.d. Widderburg
Bartek Gamla Stan	5-7-82	Igor z Zeriby	Zywia z Kordegardy
Morga z Psiego Raju	5-10-82	Gwarek z Psiego Raju	Bella z Nadwarcianskiej Doliny
King z Dobieszowic	7-19-82	Lotus Pontina	Cyra z Dobieszowic
Oda z Psiego Raju	11-18-82	Idol z Psiego Raju	Zgaga z Psiego Raju
Cezar z Henrykowa	12-4-82	Rumcajs z Jurty	Lowna z Henrykowa
Arkonia z Kordegardy	2-24-83	Hermes spod Zagla	Malwina z Kordegardy
Cizemka z Bankowcow	4-5-83	Szerszen z Zeriby	Tama Delicja
Radosz z Psiego Raju	7-7-83	Gwarek z Psiego Raju	Bella z Nadwarcianskiej Doliny
Duga Jaga z Kordegardy	7-23-83	Apasz z Bankowcow	Plaza z Kordegardy
Supel Filipon	2-14-84	Zupan z Kordegardy	Prymka z Kordegardy
Bufka spod Budy	3-26-84	Lancet z Zeriby	Niwa z Ogrodka Magdy
Brussa z Doliny Biebrzy	5-3-84	Apasz z Bankowcow	Majka z Kordegardy
Czekan Moscic	6-1-84	Igor z Zeriby	Harda z Dobieszowic
Olek v.d. Widderburg	6-30-84	Faruk v.d. Winterhaus Tuchol	Halinka v.d. Widderburg
Cynthia Arkadia	4-8-85	Lancet z Zeriby	Delta z Dobieszowic
Bart Agajax	4-15-85	King z Dobieszowic	Gera ze Starego Lupkowa
Naspa z Kordegardy	5-2-85	Apasz z Bankowcow	Malwina z Kordegardy
Orlica v.d. Raubkammer	6-26-85	Nieman v.d. Ponte Nova	Ascha Losh
Palasz z Wielgowa	11-2-85	Radosz z Psiego Raju	Garstka Saggitarius
Eddy v. Polenblut			
Ruslan Loza	4-12-86	Janosik Harnas Akribeia	Murawa Wira z Psiego Raju
Szczodra Arnika z Amieliowka	11-20-86	Czekan Moscic	Duga Jaga z Kordegardy
Bartnik z Matecznika Diany	1-26-87	Radosz z Psiego Raju	Brussa z Doliny Biebrzy
Amal Banciarnia	2-3-87	Bart Agajax	Turnia z Szalasu Puchatkow
Jedza z Matecznika Diany	11-8-87	Czekan Moscic	Brussa z Doliny Biebrzy
Vivat Pacynka	8-7-87	Supel Filipon	Kalina Rawipon
Bartosz Boruta z Matecznika Diany	1-26-87	Radosz z Psiego Raju	Brussa z Doliny Biebrzy
Irys Jukon	2-5-87	Supel Filipon	Omega Omi Ken Pol
Tymek z Amieliowki	6-7-88	Czekan Moscic	Duda Jaga z Kordegardy
Fryga Moscic	4-2-86	Czekan Moscic	Jedyna z Henrykowa
Jagoda z Matecznika Diany	11-8-87	Czekan Moscic	Brussa z Doliny Biebrzy
Kontrapunkt Lawenda	1-7-87	Kontrapunkt Ulan	Kontrapunkt Lubianka
Larysa Rawipon	3-1-88	Apasz z Bankowcow	Jemiola z Kordegardy

KENNELS IN POLAND

The following is an alphabetical listing of the better-known PON kennels that have operated from 1975 to the present in Poland.

Name	Owner	Name	Owner
Agiponik	H. Basta	Masovia	W. Szykiedans
Akribea	B. Patrzykont	Z Matecznika Diany	Z. Redlicki
Z Amieliowki	B. Wojcik	Moscic	R. Szyszkowska
Z Armii Zbawienia	J. Hudecka	Nadwarcianska Dolina	M. Gil
Baltycka Rapsodia	A. Zakrzewska	Niedzwiedzie	W. Zabicka
Z Banciarni	B. Rayska	Z Ochojca	P. Sliwka
Z Bankowcow	B. Pokorski	Od Szwajcera	M. Kaminska
Z Barnimowka	K. Marcinczyk	Ogrodek Magdy	T. Zelazny
Bonus Pastor	M. Mossler	Owczarkowa Loza	J. Falborska
Cedrowa Zagroda	J. Lewandowski	Pacynka	A. Pacyna
Complement	B. Szydlowicz-Polanczyk	Pasterskie Nstromie	J. Walczak
Delicja	G. Hallama	Pompon	L. Krzewina
Dobieszowice	O. Pawelczyk	Pontina	K. Tomaszewska
Z Doliny Olczyskiej	W. Migiel	Ponn Klup	O. Tokarska
Z Domu Marzen	T. Rzad	Psi Raj	T. Adamski
Drajkos	W. Kostanski	Psi Zawlek	J. Skoczek
Drewniana Baszta	C. Jozefacki	Rawipon	A. Romanos
Dzlabocow	Z. Hyzy	Reza	M. Zdziennicka
Dziewiata Fala	P. Kudlorz	Rod Ady	J. Zdrojek-Gromotkow
Filipon	Z. Ewertowski	Rzepicha	B. Sztajkowska
Z Gangu Dlugich	B. Larska	Sagittarius	B. Strzalkowska
Grenada	I. Krzyzanowska	Sfora Doktora	S. Chodorek
Henrykow	M. Ostenda	Skierdy	E. Marcinkowska
Hucul	K. Reder	Ze Spiewogry	A. Grabska
Inbred	M. Supronowicz	Spod Zagla	J. Wojcik
Jagniatkowo	Z. Pasterska-Glowacka	Stary Lupkow	L. Naglik
Jukon	J. Kielkiewicz	Tajemnica Poliszynela	B. Jenczyk-Tolloczko
Kawalkada	K. Babirecka	Tytus	Z. Zielinska
Ken-Pol	Z. Kaczorowska	Wesele	J. Wardyn
Koncept	Z. Jaworski	Wiejska Strzecha	W. Kalinowski
Kontrapunkt	J. Staniszewska-Borkowska	Z Wielgowa	J. Zerebecki
Kordegardy	D. Hryniewicz	Z. Wichrowej Gorki	J. Jendrczak
Kosciuszkowskie Akwarium	A. Kordylas	Winieta	Z. Mikula
Ksiezycowa	J. Olszewski	Z. Wodnikowego Lasu	T. Czyzyk
Loza	K. Jedrzejczak	Xandrina	J. Szulc
Lupczanka	A. Orlowski	Zeriba	B. Lipinska
Magna	E. Sledz		

KENNELS OUTSIDE OF POLAND

The following PON kennels were among the first to become established outside of Poland.

GERMANY

Name	Owner
Ponte Nova	E. Haase
Szymkow	M. Szymkowiak
Pon-Garten	G. Gartenschlager
Widderberg	E. Hakelberg
Sandras Pon	E. Schwerdtner
Ilsenstein	A. Neugebauer
Polenblud	R. Schielicke
Lodz	G. Dabel
Minibaren	Luft
Otti	J. Haufschild
Raubkammer	M. Schultze
Charm Zotti	Kunz
Wasantasena	S. Koppe
Domus Mira	I. Reathe
Wasantasena	S. Koppe
Hintenhaus Tuchola	S. Strong
Tierpark	Lachmann
Paerenwappen	R. Krauter

BELGIUM

Menlenhof	G. Menlen
Losch	G. Lukas
Biawa Suka	G. L. Lukas
Goralenhof	M. Jasica
Du Dre	P. M. E.v.Raresteyn

HOLLAND

White Valiant	G. Wroom
Kochana	Westernik-Lijmer
Kerberac	M. de Haas
Zonnendauw	K. van Beekstraat
Kimstanhoeve	I. W. Immers
Jestem Biata	Gelderen
Cojest	G. C. Peeters

AUSTRIA

St. Katharinen	K. Remp

DENMARK

Tieps	J. Corneliussen

UNITED STATES

Elzbieta	K. & B. Augustowski
Europa	E. J. Brown
Shaggi Pons	T.Wason & L.Shields
Rockrun	D. Zalis
Jande	J. Masters
Bur Mur	B. & M. Simberg
Von Marja	R. Rhoads & M. Von Drehle
Lechsinska	Roy & Kim Richmond

Pol. Ch. Zaspa z Wielgowa, by Ch. Radosz z Psiego Raju ex Pacyna z Wielgowa.

SKC Ch. Elzbieta's Czekolada Shagpon. Owners, Loana Shields and Tom Wason. Compared to other breeds of dog in the US, the Polski Owczarek Nizinny is often considered one of the "new kids on the block," but he is quickly making many new friends.

The PON in America

HOW RARE IT IS

Introducing a new breed into the United States is not an easy matter. The American Kennel Club currently recognizes about 140 dog breeds and varieties of dog, of which a handful of perennial favorites are solidly entrenched as America's favorite pets. To interest even a fragment of the dog owners of America in an uncommon/unknown dog breed is a significant accomplishment.

Americans are, however, predictably fascinated by the new and the different. A truly spectacular or bizarre commodity and/or an ingenious bit of marketing can spark interest in an unknown entity. The Chinese Shar-Pei, with its inordinate supply of wrinkles, dour expression, and bout with near extinction, appeared almost magically on the American dog scene in the 70s. The breed instantly whetted the public's insatiable appetite for the sublime, and commanded and received exorbitant prices for one of its kind. Breeders scrambled to accommodate the steady stream of customers who sought to be the first on their block to own the latest fad.

There are dozens of so-called rare breeds, deserving of notoriety for charm and appealing looks, that will never achieve top-ten status. The PON is one of these "undiscovered" dog breeds happy to bask in the shadow of its better-known brethren. Unbridled popularity, with all the fame and fortune that often accompanies it, is not the aim of those who have pioneered the breed in its first decade in the U.S. Rather, they seek a steady, slow, contemplative growth that perpetuates mentally and physically sound dogs.

THE POLISH CONNECTION

Betty Augustowski was not the first American to discover the cute little sheepdog with more than half of the alphabet in his name, but she was the most steadfast in her love and dedication to the breed. Others have preceded her and followed her in importing and/or breeding PONs in this country, but none have taken the welfare of this breed so passionately to heart as has Betty Augustowski. For Betty, the extra something required to stick with this lengthy, often discouraging project (promoting a rare breed that is not immune to ethnic jokes) was undoubtedly her Polish heritage.

Betty and her husband, Kaz Augustowski, are both Baltimore natives, having grown up in the Polish section of that ethnic-rich city. Honored as Slavic Woman of the Year in 1980 by the Pan Slavic National Convention, Betty has always held the traditions, the spirit, the cause of Poland dear to her heart. She and her husband had visited Poland during the Communist Era, and they kept in touch with relatives and friends despite the restrictions of the Iron Curtain.

Betty had always loved dogs, but it was not until she retired as director of sales at a large Baltimore hotel in 1975 that she channeled all her creativity and energies toward dogs. She bought some Maltese and Shih Tzus for breeding, and particularly enjoyed grooming and exhibiting her toy dogs in the show ring. The world of show dogs appealed to Betty. It gave her the opportunity to be around and be surrounded by dogs of all types. It also gave her a

longing for another dog—something really special.

It seemed strange to Betty and Kaz that they had never heard of a Polish dog breed, especially when there were so many well-known dogs from that part of the world—dogs native to Hungary, Russia,and Germany. As old and rich a culture as Poland has, they reasoned, surely there must be distinct dog breeds hidden in that ancient country. Little did they know that at the very time they were wondering about the existence of native Polish dogs, someone else had just begun the search. At the same time, Poland was leading the communist countries in opening her petals for the

Ch. Shaggi Pons Duzy Bozolski winning BOS at the 1994 National Specialty. Breeders/owners, Loana Shields (pictured) and Tom Wason. Judge, Guiseppe Alessandra. Also shown is ARBA President Betty Augustowski.

Elzbieta's Pan Vladek, the foundation dog at Elzbieta Kennels, at his first show in the US. At the age of five months, Vladek was the first Polski Owczarek Nizinny to win in an American show ring.

first time since World War II to reveal herself—her dogs, her dogma, and her direction—to the world.

ENTER PAN VLADEK

In the spring of 1982, Betty's search for her special dog ended when her husband spotted, in an American dog magazine, a small ad offering information on a Polish Lowland Sheepdog. She wrote a letter immediately, but could not wait for a reply. It didn't take her long to track down the phone number of the New York breeder who placed the ad. That phone call opened up a whole new world to Betty—and to the Polski Owczarek Nizinny.

Moira Morrison was one of the first Bearded Collie breeders in the U.S., having bred, in the late 60s, the second litter of that Scottish breed born in this country. Moira worked for full recognition of the Beardie by the AKC, and that was granted in 1977, only ten years after the first litter of Bearded Collies was born in the U.S.

Through her love of the breed, Moira researched the ancestry of the Beardie and discovered that it descended from a similar, slightly smaller but more muscular, shaggy sheepdog native to Poland.

Moira made contact with a

Int., So.Am., P.R., SKC Ch. Elzbieta's Drzowie z Rockrun. Owner/handler, Dorene Zalis. Judge, Margaret Supronowicz.

widely traveled rare-breed enthusiast in England, Muriel Landers Cooke, who further piqued Moira's interest in the PON. Muriel was writing a book about rare breeds and had visited Poland and met breeders who she thought would be willing to part with some PONs. Bundz z Starego Lupkowa and Fajerka z Kordegardy were sent to Moira Morrison in January 1979 at about eight months of age. Bundz was by Rumcajs z Juaty out of Pol. Ch. Alegoria Agiponik. Fajerka was by Pol. Ch. Turon z Psiego Raju out of Pol. Ch. Lada z Kordegardy. During the summer of 1980, three other puppies were brought to Moira; one of them was Kontrapunkt Lakotka (Figaro z Jagniatkowa and Frytka z Kordegardy). The two others were by Kaduk Tytus out of Pol. Ch. Lada z Kordegardy. Around this time, PONs were making their way into neighboring European countries, and it is known that a few came to the U.S. from Belgium and Germany via American service families and tourists.

Moira bred several litters and had one puppy left of what was to be her last litter of PONs when Betty Augustowski entered the picture. Moira was pleased to have found someone so enthusiastic about the hardy little herders from Poland.

At best count, there were only a of that offered rare breed classes. She carried copies of the breed standard with her, expounded on the little she knew about PONs, and hoped judges and exhibitors would take an interest in this new breed. Vladek attended obedience

Kaz Augustowski and Bozena Borkowska with Ch. of the Americas, Int., So.Am., P.R., SKC Ch. Mutsnah z Elzbieta; Elzbieta's Pani Von Marja; Pol., Dk. Ch. Kontrapunkt Lawenda; Zapaska Oligarchia Kawalkada; and Elzbieta's Claudius. Photo by B. Augustowski.

dozen PONs in this country in 1982 when Betty and Kaz acquired four-month-old Pan Vladek. From the moment they set eyes upon their first Polish pup, the Augustowskis, ever so proud of their Polish heritage, have zealously championed the PON and other Polish breeds in the United States.

Betty was thrilled with Vladek and didn't waste any time in showing him off. She entered him in every match or show she heard

classes, functioned as a therapy dog in nursing homes, and served as a Polish goodwill ambassador at ethnic festivals and exhibits, where he was often the star attraction.

U.S. PONS MULTIPLY

As with most people touched with the fever of purebred dog mania, Betty was not content to own only one PON. She vowed that her wonderful Vladek must live on, so she set about finding him a mate. Through their connections in Poland, the Augustowskis sought information about the breed, they contacted rare-breed groups in the U.S. hoping to find other PON owners, and they even beseeched the Polish Consul in New York for assistance in importing some of the dogs. After dozens of phone calls and letters, in the winter of 1983, Betty received word from Poland suggesting first sending her a young pair of PONs and then—even better—a pregnant bitch. In March of that same year, the precious cargo was fetched from a Canadian airport. Krymka

Elzbieta's Winston Stanley, owned by Felicia Shaw.

z Kordegardy, a gold-medal winner in Europe, gave birth the following month to five healthy PON pups—Anetka, Anolik, Plamka, Stasia and Brunek—and the Augustowskis' Elzbieta Kennels was on the map.

Unexpectedly and incredibly, Betty received a phone call in June of that same year from a pilot at Baltimore-Washington International informing her that her two dogs had arrived. Betty made a quick trip to the airport, which was near her home, and met Awans and Branka, the young pair of Kordegardy PONs that somehow got lost in trans-Atlantic translations. The Polish breeders had managed to get them on an American flight out of Germany.

In September 1983, Elzbieta Kennels' nine PONs were soon joined by Kontrapunkt Lakotka, Moira Morrison's original puppy who was now an adult. Lakotka (nicknamed "Latchka") was bred with Vladek and in April of 1984 gave birth to a litter of seven pups, which included Vladja z Elzbieta (Ski), destined to become the mother of the breed's first American champion, Europa Casimir z Elzbieta CD. A Vladek/Krymka offspring, Magda z Elzbieta, became the breed's second champion and the first PON bitch to finish.

The next addition to Elzbieta Kennels was Klon Akribeia. The nine-week-old pup was delivered from Poland in the spring of 1985. Klon brought to four the number of Elzbieta's stud dog contingency.

Int., So.Am., P.R. Ch. Zapaska Oligarchia Kawalkada, TT. Breeder, Krystyna Babirecka (Poland). Owner, Betty Augustowski.

The American PON population has flourished under the patronage of the Augustowskis. Betty and Kaz, along with a small band of dogged PON enthusiasts (Jane and Larry Brown, Dorene and Herb Zalis, Loana Shields and Tom Wason), exhibited their dogs at every opportunity. During the 1980s, the arenas open to rare breeds were scarce and sparse—at first, only casual matches where rare breeds were invited to compete and, later, at more formal States Kennel Club (SKC) shows. Although breeders of established pedigreed pooches tend to view "new kids" with a trace of disdain, and some judges fail to give minority breeds due process, PONs have slowly begun to make a mark in the dog world. By 1991, Elzbieta Kennels had produced over 200 puppies; a breed club was established; the breed had more than a dozen conformation champions, several Group and Best in Show wins to its credit, an obedience champion and three international champions; and, although not household words, Polski Owczarek Nizinny was slowly becoming familiar to many people across the country.

The American Polish Owczarek Nizinny Club (APONC) was established in 1987, and its inaugural meeting was held in October of that year. Since then, the club's membership has increased from its original eight founding members to almost 250 members. APONC is affiliated with the States Kennel Club (SKC) and is recognized by the Polish Kennel Club as the official PON parent club in America.

Ch. Europa Casimir z Elzbieta, CD going through his paces in the obedience ring with owner Loana Shields.

GOLD MEDAL WINNERS

In the fall of 1990, Betty and Kaz were invited to Poznan, Poland to receive a gold medal and honorary lifetime membership in the Polish Kennel Club for their achievements in breeding and promoting Polish dog breeds in the United States. The Augustowskis were thrilled with the citation and, as the first Americans to be so honored, considered it a significant sign of a new era of openness between Poland and America.

Pani Genowefa Ratajska of the Polish Kennel Club presenting a gold medal to Kaz and Betty Augustowski for their efforts in promoting the Polski Owczarek Nizinny in the US.

Ch. Lechsinska's Tosia, a BOB winner. In 1994, Tosia was the highest-ranking PON with ARBA. Breeder/owner, Kim Richmond. Shown by Roy Richmond. Judge, Guiseppe Alessandra. Also shown is ARBA President Betty Augustowski.

AMERICAN PONS OF NOTE

Elzbieta's Pan Vladek

(BUNDZ Z STAREGO LUPKOWA ex FAJERKA Z KORDEGARDY)

When Betty Augustowski won Best of Breed with her dog at a rare-breed match in Baltimore in October 1982, it was hardly noteworthy by the public, the press, or even the dog fancy. It was one of many such awards amassed by the Maryland dog breeder over the years. It was not a particularly big dog show, and since Betty's dog Vladek was the only one of his breed entered in the contest, it wasn't even an impressive win.

This blue ribbon did, however, represent a significant occasion for Betty and Kaz Augustowski (and for many others in retrospect), because seven-month-old Vladek was the first Polski Owczarek Nizinny to garner a recorded win in an American show ring, and his owners were as proud as punch.

Vladek was the Augustowskis' first Polish dog, the first PON to carry the Elzbieta kennel name, and the foundation stud of the breed in the U.S. More than any other single dog, Vladek influ-

Ch. Lechinska's Krol Wladyslaw, CD, TT, by Elzbieta's Beau ex Ch. Elzbieta's Rola Lenska. Owner, Cindy Czerechowicz.

enced the type and temperament of the first PONs bred in America. His name will figure prominently in the pedigrees of American champion dogs well into the future.

Vladek was a superbly structured dog, muscular and robust. Around other dogs, he was clearly the leader of the pack, yet he had a congenial rapport with people. He was intelligent, confident, and predictable. As a young dog, Vladek served as a therapy dog on visits with Betty to Baltimore nursing homes. Visitors to the

Elzbieta Kennels in the 80s were often introduced to Vladek alone, because he, due to his early socializing with the elderly, exhibited not a trace of the indifference and aloofness toward strangers apparent in most PONs.

Although Vladek had a limited show career, he sired dozens of fine dogs, including the first American conformation and obedience champion, SKC Ch. Europa Casimir z Elzbieta CD. Vladek was the sire or grandsire of nine of the first American PON champions.

To Vladek, we who love the breed owe a debt of gratitude, for it was he who so enamored the Augustowskis with his character and appearance that they undertook a campaign to promote the PON in the United States.

Krymka z Kordegardy

(KADUK OGRODEK MAGDY ex PLAZA Z KORDEGARDY)

Krymka was the second PON to take up residence at the Elzbieta Kennels in Severn, Maryland. As Vladek was Elzbieta's "top dog," Krymka must be dubbed "grande dame." She was a classy bitch, an excellent brood bitch with a classic steady PON temperament.

Before coming to the U.S, Krymka was bred with Pol. Ch. Apasz z Bankowcow in Poland and delivered five healthy pups two weeks after her arrival. For breeding purposes, the Augustowskis retained two bitches from the litter, Anetka and Anolik, and the only male, Brunek. Krymka was subsequently bred with Vladek, and they produced quality offspring, including Magda and Bobnushka, who appeared in many TV commercials. The foundation bitch upon which Elzbieta's reputation was founded, Krymka played an important part in the development of the American PON. Krymka was the mother or grandmother of seven of the first ten US champions.

Anetka and Anolik z Elzbieta

(POL. CH. APASZ Z BANKOWCOW ex KRYMKA Z KORDEGARDY)

These two females from Krymka's first litter produced many excellent puppies for Elzbieta. Of similar type, the two bitches were practically inseparable, even through maternal periods when they often tended each other's litters.

Anolik's most famous progeny (by Klon) was Int. Ch. Drobna z Elzbieta, the breed's third champion. Anetka also has many outstanding offspring to her credit, including Ch. Elzbieta's Kluska and Int., So.Am., P.R. Ch. of The Americas Mutsnah z Elzbieta.

Branka z Kordegardy

(POL., DK. CH. WACPAN Z KORDEGARDY ex MARZANNA Z KORDEGARDY)

Brunek z Elzbieta

(POL. CH. APASZ Z BANKOWCOW ex KRYMKA Z KORDEGARDY)

Branka came to the U.S. from Poland, along with Awans, at the age of three months. Brunek came from Krymka's first litter and took to Branka famously. They were bred repeatedly over the years and produced some outstanding show dogs, including Ch. Broda z Elzbieta, Ch. Elzbieta's Jazz, and Int. Ch. Elzbieta's Drzowie z Rockrun. Stud dogs Charlie and Claudius also came from these breedings.

Awans z Kordegardy

(HERMES SPOD ZAGLA ex WD., INT., POL. CH. MALWINA Z KORDEGARDY)

Awans was a handsome, pleasant-natured dog who loved the

Jane Brown with five-month-old "Ski" at the AKC Bicentennial in Philadelphia in 1984.

girls. His sense of humor and playful antics earned him the nickname of "The Clown." He was an eager obedience student and made an appearance in 1984 at the rare breed symposium in Philadelphia during the AKC centennial celebrations, hosted by the Dog Judges Association of America. Awans was used extensively at stud with various bitches, with pleasing results. Awans's children include Ch. Jande Stefan z Europa, Elzbieta's Ultimate, and Elzbieta's Oliver (outstanding obedience dog).

Kontrapunkt Lakotka

(FIGARO Z JAGNIATKOWA ex FRYTKA Z KORDEGARDY)

"Latchka" was one of Moira Morrison's original PONs. Shortly after she was brought to the U.S. in 1980, Latchka lost one of her legs after stumbling onto an animal trap. At first, it was thought that because of her disability, Latchka could not easily carry and deliver a litter of puppies. She was subsequently sold to Betty Augustowski, who sensed the bitch's intense maternal desire. With encouragement from her veterinarian, Betty bred Latchka with Vladek. The successful whelping, by Caesarian section, resulted in seven robust pups. Latchka proved to be an excellent brood bitch, seemingly grateful for the opportunity to be a mother. She blossomed at Elzbieta Kennels, running with the other PONs and all but ignoring her handicap. Her courage and good nature earned the admiration and devotion of the Augustowskis, who were devastated by her death in 1989.

Kaz Augustowski and Bozena Borkowska with Klon Akribeia; Elzbieta's Piszczka; Europa The Heirloom Marta; Zapaska Oligarchia Kawalkada; and Europa Lucia z Elzbieta. Photo by B. Augustowski.

Latchka's credits include several well-known American PONs; she was the mother of Ch. Vladja z Elzbieta, and the grandmother of four of the first ten American PON champions, including Ch. Europa Casimir z Elzbieta CD.

Klon Akribeia

(POL. CH. APASZ Z BANKOWCOW ex DUDA STARY LUPKOW)

As Latchka was probably a favorite bitch around Elzbieta kennels, it might be said that Klon was Betty Augustowski's fair-haired boy. Klon came to Elzbieta

Ch. Kluska z Elzbieta. Owner/handler, Tom Wason.

as a very young pup. He was not especially outgoing as a puppy and was slow to mature, but when fully grown mentally and physically, he developed into a very sound specimen with what Betty calls the perfect PON temperament—steady, self-assured, reliable, and non-combative. Klon passed his fine character on to his offspring who, without exception, delighted their owners with their pleasing temperaments. Klon also had several of his progeny in the "first dozen" of PON champions, including Int. Ch. Drobna z Elzbieta, Ch. Kluska z Elzbieta, Ch. Elzbieta's Czekolada Shagpon, and Ch. Elzbieta's Myle Burmar.

SKC Ch. Vladja z Elzbieta

(ELZBIETA'S PAN VLADEK ex KONTRAPUNKT LAKOTKA)

"Ski" was the first second-generation Elzbieta PON to make a name for herself. The product of a Latchka/Vladek breeding, she inherited a lot of her father's attributes, being a more feminine version of her muscular, virile sire.

Klon Akribeia at the age of four months. Owner, Betty Augustowski. Judge, James Cavallaro.

As a young dog, Ski was shown frequently at matches from Virginia to New York. Her photo was used many times in the early 1980s, for advertising the breed in dog publications and in several rare-breed books. Ski was bred

Branka z Kordegardy, dam of some of the top–winning PONs in the US.

several times by her owner, Jane Brown, with excellent results, notably the first American PON champion, Casimir.

SKC Ch. Magda z Elzbieta

(ELZBIETA'S PAN VLADEK ex KRYMKA Z KORDEGARDY)

Elzbieta Kennels considered Magda the best it had bred in its first ten years of breeding PONs. Magda was the daughter of Krymka and Vladek, and she was very much a winner from the day she was born. When she was one year old, Magda went to live with Jan Masters and became the foundation bitch of the Jande Kennels in Michigan. Magda was a showy bitch with a rich gray and white coat, excellent movement, and a typical, self-assured PON temperament. Magda ex-

SKC Ch. Magda z Elzbieta. Owners, Betty Augustowski and Janet Masters. Handled by Janet Masters. Judge, Dr. Tomasz Borkowski.

celled as a brood bitch as well as in the show ring, and her influence will be seen in the show ring for generations to come.

BIS, Int., Mex., SKC Ch. Drobna z Elzbieta

(KLON AKRIBEIA ex ANOLIK Z ELZBIETA)

"Cricket" began her show career at the age of three months, winning Best Puppy at the Baltimore Rare Breeds Match in 1986. She was subsequently seen frequently in show rings all over the East Coast. In 1989, Cricket became the first American PON to earn International and Mexican titles. Cricket's stunning jet-black coat and her outstanding movement earned her many impressive wins, including several BIS wins at rare breed shows, at the capable hands of her owner/handler Dorene Zalis.

SKC Ch. Europa Casimir z Elzbieta CD

(ELZBIETA'S PAN VLADEK ex CH. VLADJA Z ELZBIETA)

After an unfortunate beginning with a deficient owner, this dog was rescued at the age of 15 months by Loana Shields and Tom Wason of Naples, New York. With time, patience, and determination, his new owners turned "Cas" into a physically and mentally superior dog. He became, in 1987, the first American PON conformation champion. In 1990, Cas made history again when he completed the third leg of his obedience championship, making him the first American PON to achieve that honor. Cas was no stranger to SKC show rings in the Midwest, on the East Coast, and in the South; and his owners played an integral part in establishing the breed in its early days in the U.S.

Betty and Kaz Augustowski with puppy "Misha."

Every PON enjoys the opportunity to be outdoors. Basking in the sun is Bolek, owned by Jane I. Tryniszewski.

BIS, Int., So.Am., P.R., SKC Ch. Elzbieta's Drzowie z Rockrun

(BRUNEK Z ELZBIETA ex BRANKA Z KORDEGARDY)

"Zoe" is the top winning PON show dog in the United States, and it is doubtful whether another PON could surpass her record of show wins in the next decade.

Before Zoe came on the scene, American PONs had encountered little success in all-breed competitions. PON owners came to realize that, if there is one place that a PON does not shine, it's in a show ring. Surely, if a PON could talk, he would tell his master, "I don't like showing—I'd rather be home, but I'll do it if I have to." This is the attitude and this is the demeanor of a typical PON in a show ring.

With her second PON, Dorene Zalis took up the challenge. From the beginning, Zoe learned to enjoy the rigors of grooming and

GROUP FIRST
PUPPY
AMERICAN
RARE BREED ASSN.
ORANGE BLOSSOM
CLASSIC
SUN. P M SHOW
1994 BRUCE HARKINS

Winning puppy. Elzbieta's Precious Kaitlin with proud owner Merrilee Finch.

showing. The end product was an extraordinary PON bitch with a luxurious cream coat, a flamboyant personality and a string of Best in Show wins. The elegant Zoe was indeed a show stopper and must be credited with propelling the Polski Owczarek Nizinny into the American limelight.

SKC Ch. Inbred Lapowka

(CH. PALASZ Z WIELGOWA ex LETA Z KORDEGARDY)

Lapowka came to the U.S. in 1989 with her breeder/owners Dr. Margaret Supronowicz and Dr. Tomasz Borkowski. She was shown in Poland a few times and won a Junior Winner title and a Polish Kennel Club Certificate of Merit, but was too young to achieve her championship under Poland's stringent rules. Lapowka has become an SKC Champion and took Best of Breed at the first APONC National Specialty in May 1992.

One of Lapowka's breedings with Vladek produced an outstanding black and white male, Elzbieta's Polski Duma, who easily attained his championships

Int., So.Am., P.R., SKC Ch. Elzbieta's Drzowie z Rockrun. Owner/handler, Dorene Zalis. Judge, Betty Augustowski.

and is probably the most-titled PON in the world: Int., So.Am., P.R. Ch. of the Americas, SKC Ch. Elzbieta's Polski Duma.

Dk., Pol. Ch. Kontrapunkt Lawenda

(KONTRAPUNKT ULAN ex LUBIANKA Z KORDEGARDY)

In November 1991, the Augustowskis imported the first Polish and Danish champion into the United States. Lawenda was extremely gentle and very typical of a sound PON bitch. She brought ten gold medals from Europe with her.

Premier Oligarchia

(KUSY KAWALKADA ex VENA PACYNKA)

In January 1992, Premier came to the U.S. from Poland for a few weeks to be bred to Lapowka and Elzbieta's Ciena, a daughter of Vladek and Lapowka. Prior to this journey, the 16-month-old Pre-

Future champion Elzbieta's Polski Duma at five months of age. Owners, Dorene Zalis and Betty Augustowski.

mier had many Junior Winner titles and a junior class BOB from a European dog show in Finland.

A working PON is a happy PON. Two PONs from Kontrapunkt Kennels have this herd of goats well under control. Photo by B. Augustowski.

Ch. of the Americas, Int., So. Am., P.R., SKC Ch. Mutsnah z Elzbieta

(ELZBIETA'S PAN VLADEK ex ANETKA Z ELZBIETA)

Mutsnah, whose name translates to "strong" in English, was the first puppy born in her litter. In a state of confusion, Anetka, Mutsnah's mother, accidentally lifted the scalp off of her newborn. The puppy was rushed to the animal hospital, where its scalp was stitched back on at the age of 15 minutes. There was little hope for the puppy's survival, but she fooled everyone. Mutsnah's injury healed without a problem, which is how she got her name. Mutsnah is also a very capable herder, moving ducks and geese to their areas each evening.

NEW POLISH IMPORTS

When Betty Augustowski returned from Poland in June 1992, she brought three PONs of other bloodlines: Zapaska Oligarchia Kawalkada (Pol. Ch. Tymek z Ameliowki ex Hesia Krysiow), a female that she and her husband now own; Kontrapunkt Rozgrywka (Zwiron Kontrapunkt ex Tjeps PON Figlarka, a female now owned by Mary E. Von Drehle; and Kontrapunkt Ryzykant (Zwiron Kontrapunkt ex Tjeps PON Figlarka), a male now owned by Carol Niles.

The CACIB (Certificate of Aptitude for Championship of International Beauty) awarded by the Federation Cynologique internationale (FCI) to Ch. of the Americas, Int., So.Am., P.R., SKC Ch. Mutsnah z Elzbieta.

Ch. of the Americas, Int., So.Am., P.R., SKC Ch. Mutsnah z Elzbieta. Owner, Betty Augustowski. Judge, Dr. Mario Perricone.

FIRST AMERICAN PON CHAMPIONS

SKC CH. EUROPA CASIMIR Z ELZBIETA
   Date of Championship: 10/88
   Sire: Elzbieta's Pan Vladek
   Dam: Ch. Vladja z Elzbieta

SKC CH. MAGDA Z ELZBIETA
   Date of Championship: 2/89
   Sire: Elzbieta's Pan Vladek
   Dam: Krymka z Kordegardy

INT., MEX., SKC CH. DROBNA Z ELZBIETA
   DATE OF Championship: 7/89
   Sire: Klon Akribeia
   Dam: Anolik z Elzbieta

SKC CH. JANDE STEFAN Z EUROPA
   Date of Championship: 11/89
   Sire: Awans z Kordegardy
   Dam: Ch. Vladja z Elzbieta

SKC CH. KLUSKA Z ELZBIETA
  Date of Championship: 12/89
  Sire: Klon Akribeia
  Dam: Anetka z Elzbieta

SKC CH. VLADJA Z ELZBIETA
  Date of Championship: 4/90
  Sire: Elzbieta's Pan Vladek
  Dam: Kontrapunkt Lakotka

INT., SO.AM., P.R., SKC CH.
ELZBIETA'S DRZOWIE Z
ROCKRUN
  Date of Championship: 7/90
  Sire: Brunek z Elzbieta
  Dam: Branka z Kordegardy

SKC Ch. Europa Casimir z Elzbieta, CD. Owner/handler, Loana Shields.

Elzbieta's Bear. Owners, John and Joni Stevens.

SKC CH. ELZBIETA'S MYLE
BURMAR
  Date of Championship: 11/90
  Sire: Klon Akribeia
  Dam: Marny z Elzbieta

SKC CH. BRODA Z ELZBIETA
  Date of Championship: 11/90
  Sire: Brunek z Elzbieta
  Dam: Branka z Kordegardy

SKC CH. ELZBIETA'S
CZEKOLADA SHAGPON
  Date of Championship: 11/90
  Sire: Klon z Akribeia
  Dam: Marny z Elzbieta

SKC CH. JANDE JAJANNA
ELZBIETA
  Date of Championship: 7/91
  Sire: Elzbieta's Claudius
  Dam: Ch. Magda z Elzbieta

SKC CH. ELZBIETA'S POLISH JAZZ
   Date of Championship: 8/91
   Sire: Brunek z Elzbieta
   Dam: Branka z Kordegardy

CH. OF THE AMERICAS, INT., SO. AM., P.R., SKC CH. ELZBIETA'S POLSKI DUMA
   Date of Championship: 5/92
   Sire: Elzbieta's Pan Vladek
   Dam: Inbred Lapowka

CH. OF THE AMERICAS, INT., SO. AM., P.R., SKC CH. MUTSNAH Z ELZBIETA
   Date of Championship: 5/92
   Sire: Elzbieta's Pan Vladek
   Dam: Anetka z Elzbieta

SKC Ch. Elzbieta's Myle z Burmar. Owner/handler, Bert Simberg.

"Hannah," a BOS winner. Owner, Susan Stekoll.

SKC CH. INBRED LAPOWKA
   Date of Championship: 6/92
   Sire: Ch. Palasz z Wielgowa
   Dam: Leta z Kordegardy

Ch. Cosmos Tarok Bator, by Tarok ex Duszka. Owner, M.L. Cumming. Breeder, Lynne Colquhoun Zubrzycki.

Ch. Ponwood's Esther Ofarim, by Archy–Pon von–Ascona ex Ponwood's Bella. Owner, Nancy Gardzelewski. Breeders, Barbara Bruns and Wolfgang Stamp (Germany).

Pedigrees of Foundation PONs

A pedigree, as defined by the American Kennel Club, is "the written record of a dog's geneology for three generations or more." The following collection of pedigrees represents the most important foundation Polski Owczarek Nizinnies from both Poland and America. Serving as a definitive way to study the means and inspiration of Polish and American breeders over past decades, these pedigrees prove invaluable in tracing the history of specific PON lines not only in Poland but also in all other countries with established lines. The first 16 pages of this chapter contain pedigrees of Polish dogs, followed by 11 pages of significant American pedigrees.

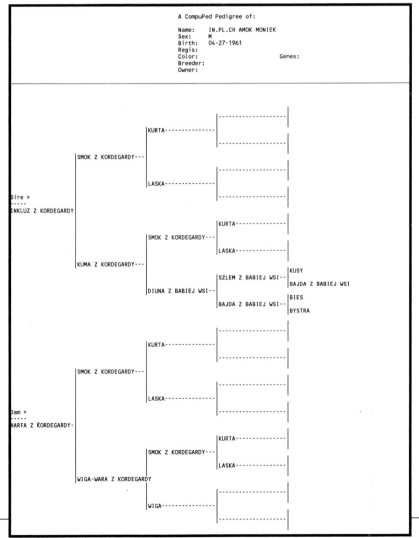

```
A CompuPed Pedigree of:

Name:    IN.PL.CH AMOK MONIEK
Sex:     M
Birth:   04-27-1961
Regis:
Color:                          Genes:
Breeder:
Owner:


                                     KURTA---------------  --------------------
                                                           --------------------
                      SMOK Z KORDEGARDY---
                                     LASKA---------------  --------------------
                                                           --------------------
  Sire >
  -----
  INKLUZ Z KORDEGARDY
                                     SMOK Z KORDEGARDY---  KURTA---------------
                                                           LASKA---------------
                      KUMA Z KORDEGARDY---
                                                           SZLEM Z BABIEJ WSI--|KUSY
                                     DIUNA Z BABIEJ WSI--                      |BAJDA Z BABIEJ WSI
                                                           BAJDA Z BABIEJ WSI--|BIES
                                                                               |BYSTRA

                                     KURTA---------------  --------------------
                                                           --------------------
                      SMOK Z KORDEGARDY---
                                     LASKA---------------  --------------------
                                                           --------------------
  Dam >
  -----
  HARFA Z KORDEGARDY-
                                     SMOK Z KORDEGARDY---  KURTA---------------
                                                           LASKA---------------
                      WIGA-WARA Z KORDEGARDY
                                     WIGA----------------  --------------------
                                                           --------------------
```

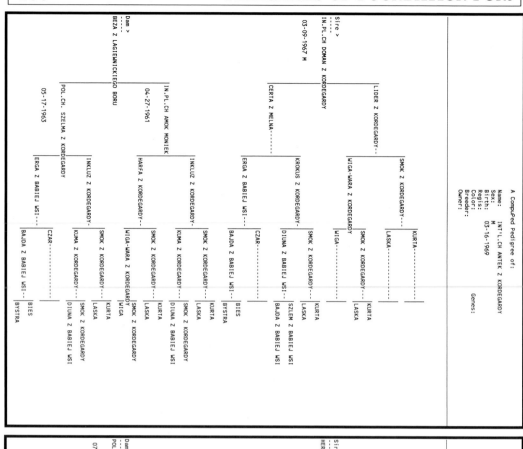

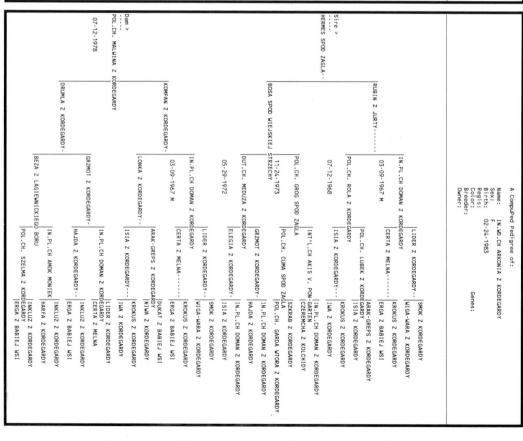

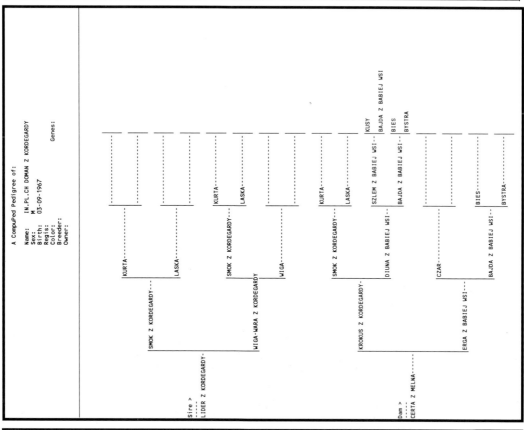

A CompuPed Pedigree of:

Name: IN.PL.CH DOMAN Z KORDEGARDY
Sex: M
Birth: 03-09-1967
Regis:
Color:
Breeder:
Owner: Genes:

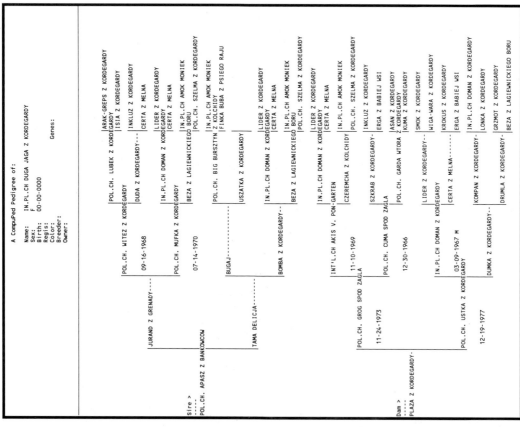

A CompuPed Pedigree of:

Name: IN.PL.CH DUGA JAGA Z KORDEGARDY
Sex: F
Birth: 00-00-0000
Regis:
Color:
Breeder:
Owner: Genes:

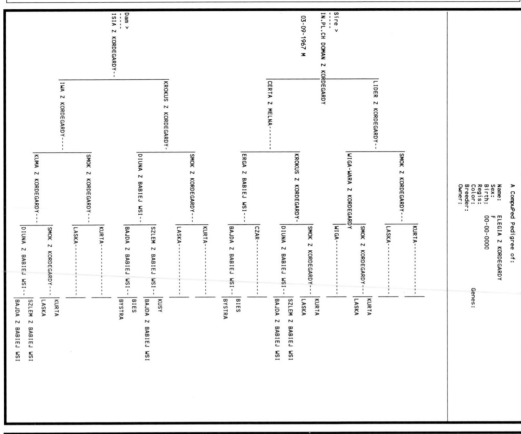

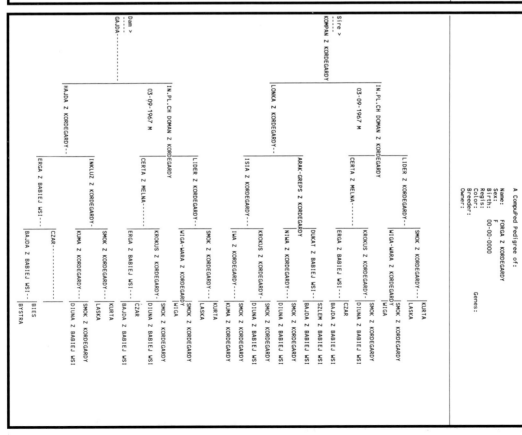

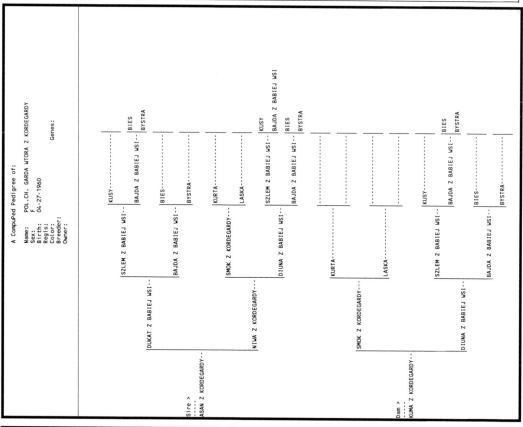

A CompuPed Pedigree of:

Name: POL.CH. GARDA WTORA Z KORDEGARDY
Sex: F
Birth: 04-27-1960
Regis:
Color:
Breeder:
Owner:

Genes:

Sire >
ASAN Z KORDEGARDY--

DUKAT Z BABIEJ WSI--

SZLEM Z BABIEJ WSI--

KUSY--

BAJDA Z BABIEJ WSI--

BIES
BYSTRA

BAJDA Z BABIEJ WSI--

BIES--
BYSTRA--

NINA Z KORDEGARDY--

SMOK Z KORDEGARDY--

KURTA--
LASKA--

DIUNA Z BABIEJ WSI--

SZLEM Z BABIEJ WSI--
BAJDA Z BABIEJ WSI--

KUSY--
BIES
BYSTRA

Dam >
KUMA Z KORDEGARDY--

SMOK Z KORDEGARDY--

KURTA--
LASKA--

SZLEM Z BABIEJ WSI--
BAJDA Z BABIEJ WSI--

KUSY--
BIES
BYSTRA

DIUNA Z BABIEJ WSI--

BAJDA Z BABIEJ WSI--

BIES--
BYSTRA--

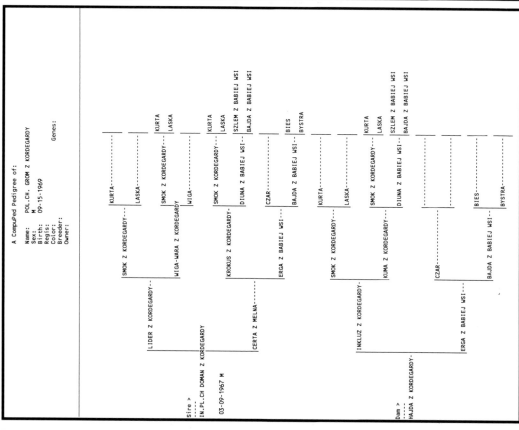

A CompuPed Pedigree of:

Name: POL.CH. GROM Z KORDEGARDY
Sex: M
Birth: 09-15-1969
Regis:
Color:
Breeder:
Owner:

Genes:

Sire >
-----IN.PL.CH DOMAN Z KORDEGARDY

03-09-1967 M

LIDER Z KORDEGARDY--

SMOK Z KORDEGARDY--

KURTA--
LASKA--

WIGA-WARA Z KORDEGARDY

SMOK Z KORDEGARDY--
WIGA--

KURTA
LASKA

CERTA Z MELNA-----

KROKUS Z KORDEGARDY-

SMOK Z KORDEGARDY-
DIUNA Z BABIEJ WSI--

KURTA
LASKA
SZLEM Z BABIEJ WSI
BAJDA Z BABIEJ WSI

ERGA Z BABIEJ WSI--

CZAR--
BAJDA Z BABIEJ WSI--

BIES
BYSTRA

Dam >
-----HAJDA Z KORDEGARDY-

INKLUZ Z KORDEGARDY-

SMOK Z KORDEGARDY--

KURTA--
LASKA--

KUMA Z KORDEGARDY--

SMOK Z KORDEGARDY--
DIUNA Z BABIEJ WSI--

KURTA
LASKA
SZLEM Z BABIEJ WSI
BAJDA Z BABIEJ WSI

ERGA Z BABIEJ WSI--

CZAR--
BAJDA Z BABIEJ WSI--

BIES--
BYSTRA--

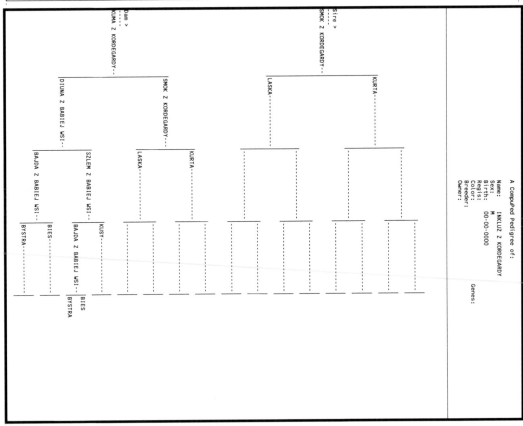

A CompuPed Pedigree of:

Name: INKLUZ Z KORDEGARDY
Sex: M
Birth:
Regis: 00-00-0000
Color:
Breeder:
Owner:

Genes:

Sire > SMOK Z KORDEGARDY

Dam > KUMA Z KORDEGARDY--

KURTA--

LASKA--

SMOK Z KORDEGARDY--

DIUNA Z BABIEJ WSI--

KURTA--

LASKA--

SZLEM Z BABIEJ WSI--

BAJDA Z BABIEJ WSI--

KUSY-

BIES

BAJDA Z BABIEJ WSI--

BIES

BYSTRA

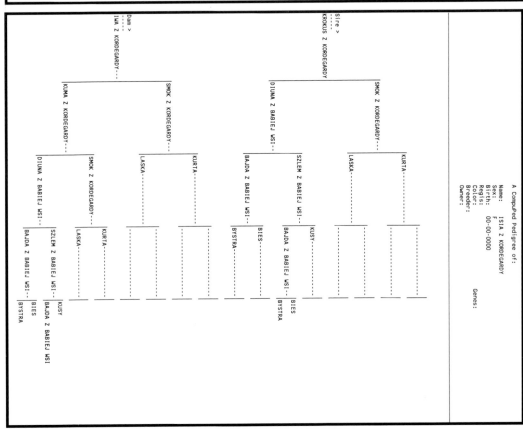

A CompuPed Pedigree of:

Name: ISIA Z KORDEGARDY
Sex: F
Birth:
Regis: 00-00-0000
Color:
Breeder:
Owner:

Genes:

Sire > KROKUS Z KORDEGARDY

Dam > IWA Z KORDEGARDY--

SMOK Z KORDEGARDY--

DIUNA Z BABIEJ WSI--

SMOK Z KORDEGARDY--

KUMA Z KORDEGARDY--

KURTA--

LASKA--

SZLEM Z BABIEJ WSI--

BAJDA Z BABIEJ WSI--

KURTA--

LASKA--

DIUNA Z BABIEJ WSI--

KUSY-

BIES

BAJDA Z BABIEJ WSI--

BIES

BYSTRA

KURTA---

LASKA---

SZLEM Z BABIEJ WSI--

BAJDA Z BABIEJ WSI--

BAJDA Z BABIEJ WSI--

KUSY

BIES

BAJDA Z BABIEJ WSI

BIES

BYSTRA

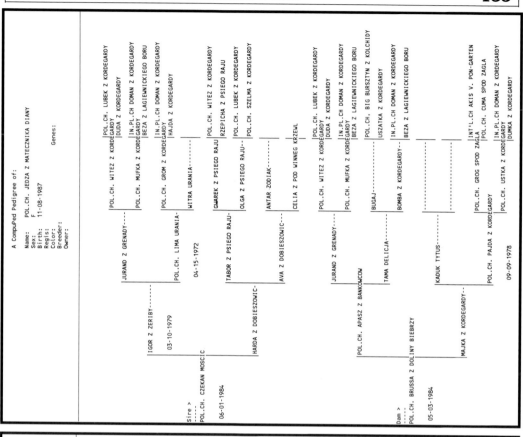

A CompuPed Pedigree of:

Name: POL.CH. JEDZA Z MATECZNIKA DIANY
Sex: F
Birth: 11-08-1987
Regis:
Color: Genes:
Breeder:
Owner:

Sire >
POL.CH. CZEKAN MOSCIC
06-01-1984

IGOR Z ZERIBY
03-10-1979

JURAND Z GRENADY

POL.CH. WITEZ Z KORDEGARDY
POL.CH. LUBEK Z KORDEGARDY
DUDA Z KORDEGARDY

POL.CH. MUFKA Z KORDEGARDY
IN.PL.CH DOMAN Z KORDEGARDY
BEZA Z LAGIEWNICKIEGO BORU

POL.CH. LIMA URANIA-
04-15-1972

POL.CH. GROM Z KORDEGARDY
IN.PL.CH DOMAN Z KORDEGARDY
HAJDA Z KORDEGARDY

WITRA URANIA-

HARDA Z DOBIESZOWIC-

TABOR Z PSIEGO RAJU

GWAREK Z PSIEGO RAJU
POL.CH. WITEZ Z KORDEGARDY
RZEPICHA Z PSIEGO RAJU

OLGA Z PSIEGO RAJU-
POL.CH. LUBEK Z KORDEGARDY
POL.CH. SZELMA Z KORDEGARDY

AVA Z DOBIESZOWIC-

ANTAR ZODIAK-

CELIA Z POD WINNEG KRZEWL

Dam >
POL.CH. BRUSSA Z DOLINY BIEBRZY
05-03-1984

POL.CH. APASZ Z BANKOWCOW

JURAND Z GRENADY

POL.CH. WITEZ Z KORDEGARDY
POL.CH. LUBEK Z KORDEGARDY
DUDA Z KORDEGARDY

POL.CH. MUFKA Z KORDEGARDY
IN.PL.CH DOMAN Z KORDEGARDY
BEZA Z LAGIEWNICKIEGO BORU

TAMA DELICJA-

BUGAJ-
POL.CH. BIG BURSZTYN Z KOLCHIDY
USZATKA Z KORDEGARDY

BOMBA Z KORDEGARDY-
IN.PL.CH DOMAN Z KORDEGARDY
BEZA Z LAGIEWNICKIEGO BORU

MAJKA Z KORDEGARDY--
09-09-1978

KADUK TYTUS-

INT'L.CH AKIS V. PON-GARTEN
POL.CH. GROG SPOD ZAGLA
POL.CH. CUMA SPOD ZAGLA

POL.CH. PAJDA Z KORDEGARDY
IN.PL.CH DOMAN Z KORDEGARDY
POL.CH. USTKA Z KORDEGARDY
DUMKA Z KORDEGARDY

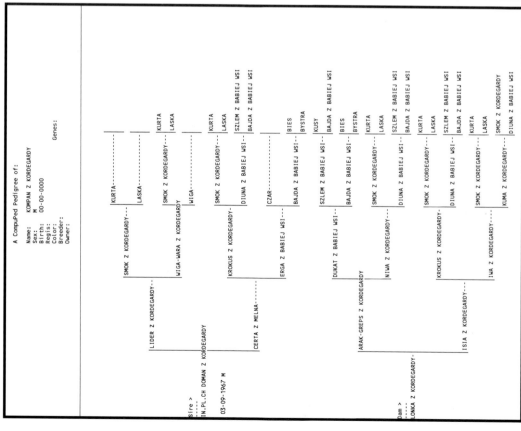

A CompuPed Pedigree of:

Name: KOMPAN Z KORDEGARDY
Sex: M
Birth: 00-00-0000
Regis:
Color: Genes:
Breeder:
Owner:

Sire >
IN.PL.CH DOMAN Z KORDEGARDY
03-09-1967 M

LIDER Z KORDEGARDY--

SMOK Z KORDEGARDY---

KURTA
LASKA

WIGA-WARA Z KORDEGARDY
SMOK Z KORDEGARDY
WIGA

CERTA Z MELNA------

KROKUS Z KORDEGARDY-
KURTA
LASKA

DIUNA Z BABIEJ WSI-
SZLEM Z BABIEJ WSI
BAJDA Z BABIEJ WSI

ERGA Z BABIEJ WSI---
CZAR-
BIES
BYSTRA

BAJDA Z BABIEJ WSI--
KUSY
BAJDA Z BABIEJ WSI

Dam >
LONKA Z KORDEGARDY-

ARAK-GREPS Z KORDEGARDY

DUKAT Z BABIEJ WSI--
SZLEM Z BABIEJ WSI
BIES
BYSTRA

NIWA Z KORDEGARDY---
SMOK Z KORDEGARDY-
KURTA
LASKA

DIUNA Z BABIEJ WSI-
SZLEM Z BABIEJ WSI
BAJDA Z BABIEJ WSI

ISIA Z KORDEGARDY---

KROKUS Z KORDEGARDY-
SMOK Z KORDEGARDY-
KURTA
LASKA

DIUNA Z BABIEJ WSI-
SZLEM Z BABIEJ WSI
BAJDA Z BABIEJ WSI

IWA Z KORDEGARDY----
SMOK Z KORDEGARDY
KURTA
LASKA

KUMA Z KORDEGARDY-
SMOK Z KORDEGARDY
DIUNA Z BABIEJ WSI

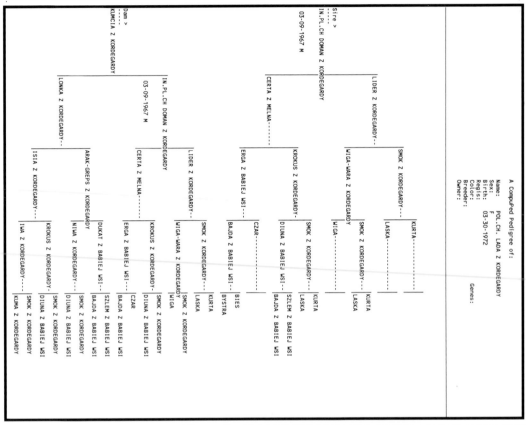

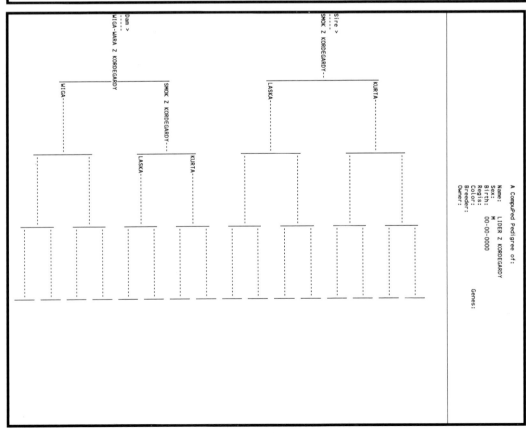

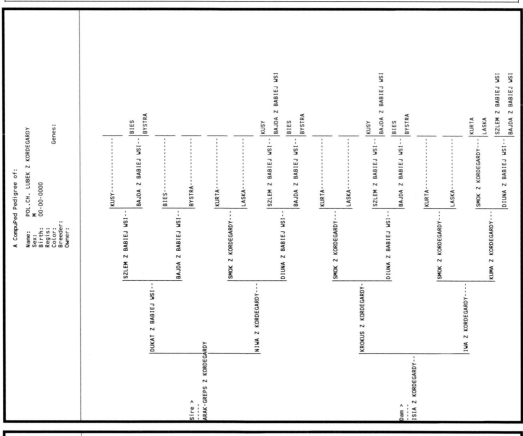

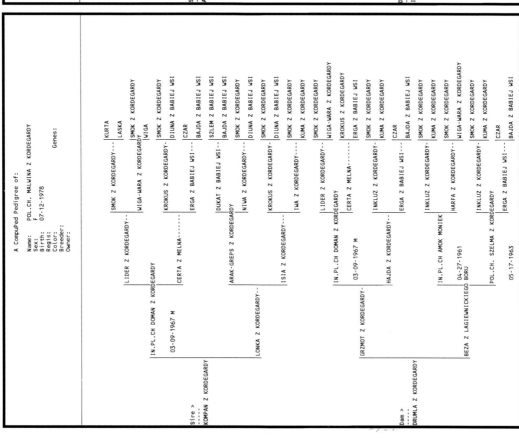

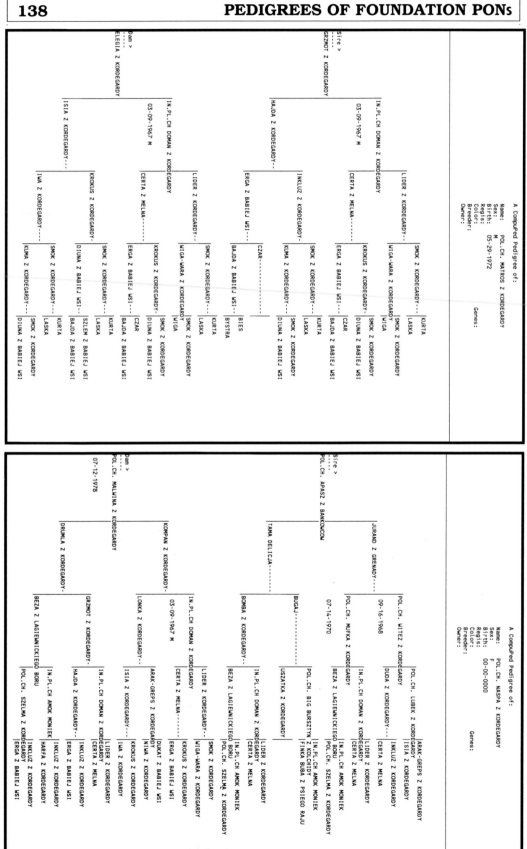

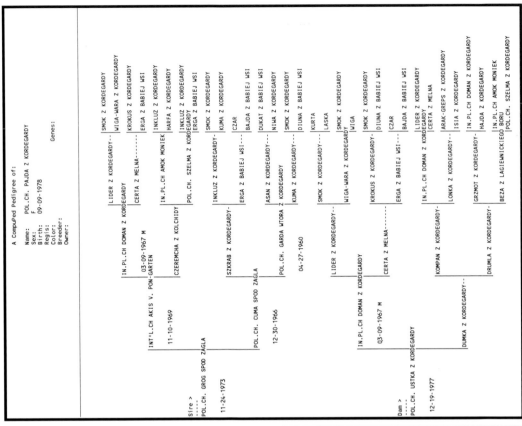

A CompuPed Pedigree of:

```
Name:    POL.CH. PAJDA Z KORDEGARDY
Sex:     F
Birth:   09-09-1978
Regis:
Color:
Breeder:
Owner:                      Genes:
```

Sire >

POL.CH. GROG SPOD ZAGLA

```
                    IN.PL.CH DOMAN Z KORDEGARDY
                    03-09-1967 M
INT'L.CH AKIS V. PON-GARTEN
11-10-1969
CZEREMCHA Z KOLCHIDY

                    SZKRAB Z KORDEGARDY-
11-24-1973
POL.CH. CUMA SPOD ZAGLA

                    POL.CH. GARDA WTORA Z
12-30-1966
                    04-27-1960
```

```
LIDER Z KORDEGARDY----|SMOK Z KORDEGARDY
                      |WIGA-WARA Z KORDEGARDY
CERTA Z MELNA---------|KROKUS Z KORDEGARDY
                      |ERGA Z BABIEJ WSI
                      |INKLUZ Z KORDEGARDY
IN.PL.CH AMOK MONIEK  |HARFA Z KORDEGARDY
                      |INKLUZ Z KORDEGARDY
POL.CH. SZELMA Z KORDEGARDY
                      |ERGA Z BABIEJ WSI
INKLUZ Z KORDEGARDY---|SMOK Z KORDEGARDY
                      |KUMA Z KORDEGARDY
ERGA Z BABIEJ WSI-----|CZAR
                      |BAJDA Z BABIEJ WSI
ASAN Z KORDEGARDY-----|DUKAT Z BABIEJ WSI
                      |NIWA Z KORDEGARDY
KUMA Z KORDEGARDY-----|SMOK Z KORDEGARDY
                      |DIUNA Z BABIEJ WSI
```

Dam >

POL.CH. USTKA Z KORDEGARDY
12-19-1977

```
                    IN.PL.CH DOMAN Z KORDEGARDY
                    03-09-1967 M
POL.CH. USTKA Z KORDEGARDY

KOMPAN Z KORDEGARDY-
DUMKA Z KORDEGARDY-
DRUMLA Z KORDEGARDY-
```

```
LIDER Z KORDEGARDY----|SMOK Z KORDEGARDY
                      |KURTA
                      |LASKA
                      |SMOK Z KORDEGARDY
WIGA-WARA Z KORDEGARDY|WIGA
KROKUS Z KORDEGARDY---|SMOK Z KORDEGARDY
                      |DIUNA Z BABIEJ WSI
CERTA Z MELNA---------|CZAR
                      |BAJDA Z BABIEJ WSI
ERGA Z BABIEJ WSI-----|LIDER Z KORDEGARDY
                      |CERTA Z MELNA
IN.PL.CH DOMAN Z KORDEGARDY|ARAK-GREPS Z KORDEGARDY
                      |ISIA Z KORDEGARDY
LONKA Z KORDEGARDY----|IN.PL.CH DOMAN Z KORDEGARDY
GRZMOT Z KORDEGARDY---|HAJDA Z KORDEGARDY
                      |IN.PL.CH AMOK MONIEK
BEZA Z LAGIEWNICKIEGO BORU|POL.CH. SZELMA Z KORDEGARDY
```

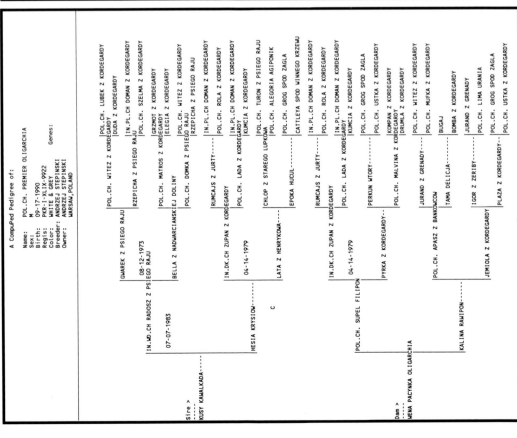

A CompuPed Pedigree of:

```
Name:    POL.CH. PREMIER OLIGARCHIA
Sex:     M
Birth:   09-17-1990
Regis:   PKR-I-XLIX-9922
Color:   WHITE & GREY
Breeder: ANDRZEJ STEPINSKI
Owner:   ANDRZEJ STEPINSKI
         WARSAW,POLAND          Genes:
```

Sire >

KUSY KAWALKADA-----

```
                    GWAREK Z PSIEGO RAJU
                    08-12-1973
IN.WD.CH RADOSZ Z PSIEGO RAJU
07-07-1983
BELLA Z MADWARCIANSKIEJ DOLINY

                    IN.DK.CH ZUPAN Z KORDEGARDY
                    04-14-1979
HESIA KRYSIOM------
         C
LATA Z HENRYKOWA----
```

```
POL.CH. WITEZ Z KORDEGARDY----|POL.CH. LUBEK Z KORDEGARDY
                              |DUDA Z KORDEGARDY
RZEPICHA Z PSIEGO RAJU--------|IN.PL.CH DOMAN Z KORDEGARDY
                              |POL.CH. SZELMA Z KORDEGARDY
POL.CH. MATROS Z KORDEGARDY---|GRZMOT Z KORDEGARDY
                              |ELEGIA Z KORDEGARDY
POL.CH. DOMKA Z PSIEGO RAJU---|POL.CH. WITEZ Z KORDEGARDY
                              |RZEPICHA Z PSIEGO RAJU
RUMCAJS Z JURTY---------------|IN.PL.CH DOMAN Z KORDEGARDY
                              |POL.CH. ROLA Z KORDEGARDY
POL.CH. LADA Z KORDEGARDY-----|IN.PL.CH DOMAN Z KORDEGARDY
                              |KUMCIA Z KORDEGARDY
CHLOP Z STAREGO LUPKOWA-------|POL.CH. TURON Z PSIEGO RAJU
                              |POL.CH. ALEGORIA AGIPONIK
EPOKA HUCUL------------------|POL.CH. GROG SPOD ZAGLA
                              |CATTLEYA SPOD WINNEGO KRZEWU
```

Dam >

WENA PACYNKA OLIGARCHIA

```
                    POL.CH. SUPEL FILIPON
PYRKA Z KORDEGARDY--
KALINA RAWIPON-----
                    POL.CH. APASZ Z BANKOWCOW
JEMIOLA Z KORDEGARDY
```

```
RUMCAJS Z JURTY---------------|IN.PL.CH DOMAN Z KORDEGARDY
                              |POL.CH. ROLA Z KORDEGARDY
POL.CH. LADA Z KORDEGARDY-----|IN.PL.CH DOMAN Z KORDEGARDY
                              |KUMCIA Z KORDEGARDY
PERKUN WTORY------------------|POL.CH. GROG SPOD ZAGLA
                              |POL.CH. USTKA Z KORDEGARDY
POL.CH. MALVINA Z KORDEGARDY--|KOMPAN Z KORDEGARDY
                              |DRUMLA Z KORDEGARDY
JURAND Z GRENADY--------------|POL.CH. WITEZ Z KORDEGARDY
                              |POL.CH. MUFKA Z KORDEGARDY
TAMA DELICJA-----------------|BUGAJ
                              |BOMBA Z KORDEGARDY
IGOR Z ZERIBY----------------|JURAND Z GRENADY
                              |POL.CH. LIMA URANIA
PLAZA Z KORDEGARDY-----------|POL.CH. GROG SPOD ZAGLA
                              |POL.CH. USTKA Z KORDEGARDY
```

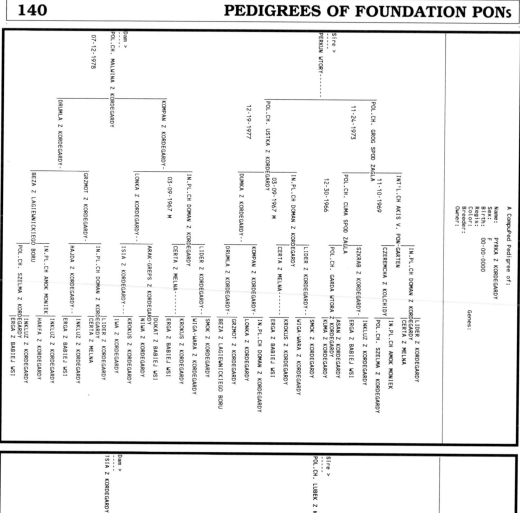

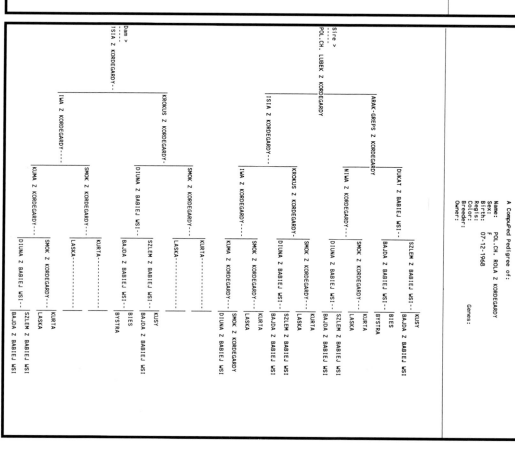

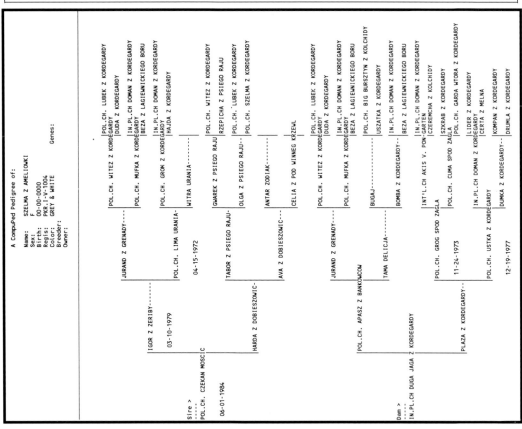

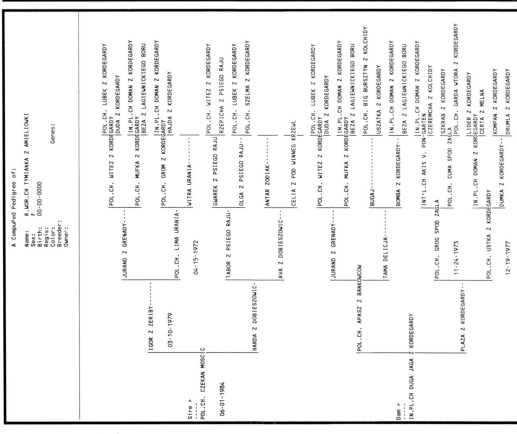

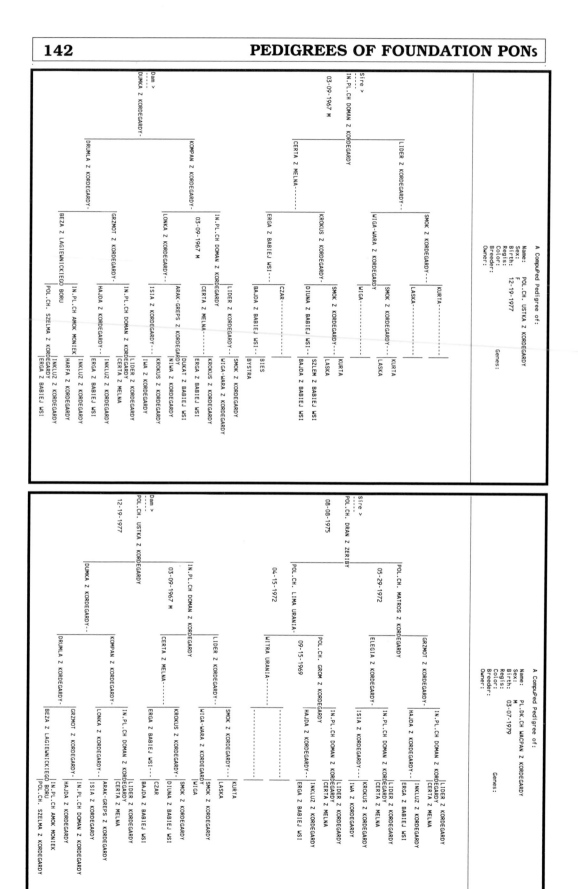

A Computed Pedigree of:

Name: POL.CH. USTKA Z KORDEGARDY
Sex: F
Birth: 12-19-1977
Regis:
Color:
Breeder:
Owner:
Genes:

Sire >
IN.PL.CH DOMAN Z KORDEGARDY
03-09-1967 M

- LIDER Z KORDEGARDY
  - SMOK Z KORDEGARDY
    - KURTA
    - LASKA
  - WIGA-WARA Z KORDEGARDY
    - SMOK Z KORDEGARDY — KURTA / LASKA
    - WIGA
- CERTA Z MELNA
  - KROKUS Z KORDEGARDY
    - SMOK Z KORDEGARDY — KURTA / LASKA
    - DIUNA Z BABIEJ WSI — SZLEM Z BABIEJ WSI / BAJDA Z BABIEJ WSI
  - ERGA Z BABIEJ WSI
    - CZAR — BIES / BYSTRA
    - BAJDA Z BABIEJ WSI

Dam >
DUMKA Z KORDEGARDY

- KOMPAN Z KORDEGARDY
  03-09-1967 M
  - IN.PL.CH DOMAN Z KORDEGARDY
    - LIDER Z KORDEGARDY — SMOK Z KORDEGARDY / WIGA-WARA Z KORDEGARDY
    - CERTA Z MELNA — KROKUS Z KORDEGARDY / ERGA Z BABIEJ WSI
  - LONKA Z KORDEGARDY
    - ARAK-GREPS Z KORDEGARDY — DUKAT Z BABIEJ WSI / NIWA Z KORDEGARDY
    - ISIA Z KORDEGARDY — KROKUS Z KORDEGARDY / IWA Z KORDEGARDY
- DRUMLA Z KORDEGARDY
  - GRZMOT Z KORDEGARDY
    - IN.PL.CH DOMAN Z KORDEGARDY — LIDER Z KORDEGARDY / CERTA Z MELNA
    - HAJDA Z KORDEGARDY — LIDER Z KORDEGARDY / ERGA Z BABIEJ WSI
  - BEZA Z LAGIEWNICKIEGO BORU
    - IN.PL.CH AMOK MONIEK — INKLUZ Z KORDEGARDY / HARFA Z KORDEGARDY
    - POL.CH. SZELMA Z KORDEGARDY — INKLUZ Z KORDEGARDY / ERGA Z BABIEJ WSI

A Computed Pedigree of:

Name: POL.DK.CH WACPAN Z KORDEGARDY
Sex: M
Regis:
Birth: 03-07-1979
Color:
Breeder:
Owner:
Genes:

Sire >
POL.CH. DRAN Z ZERIBY
08-08-1975

- POL.CH. MATROS Z KORDEGARDY
  05-29-1972
  - GRZMOT Z KORDEGARDY
    - IN.PL.CH DOMAN Z KORDEGARDY — LIDER Z KORDEGARDY / CERTA Z MELNA
    - HAJDA Z KORDEGARDY — LIDER Z KORDEGARDY / ERGA Z BABIEJ WSI
  - ELEGIA Z KORDEGARDY
    - ISIA Z KORDEGARDY — KROKUS Z KORDEGARDY / IWA Z KORDEGARDY
    - IN.PL.CH DOMAN Z KORDEGARDY — LIDER Z KORDEGARDY / CERTA Z MELNA
- POL.CH. LIMA URANIA
  04-15-1972
  - POL.CH. GROM Z KORDEGARDY
    09-15-1969
    - IN.PL.CH DOMAN Z KORDEGARDY — SMOK Z KORDEGARDY / WIGA
    - HAJDA Z KORDEGARDY — INKLUZ Z KORDEGARDY / ERGA Z BABIEJ WSI
  - WITRA URANIA

Dam >
POL.CH. USTKA Z KORDEGARDY
12-19-1977

- IN.PL.CH DOMAN Z KORDEGARDY
  03-09-1967 M
  - LIDER Z KORDEGARDY
    - SMOK Z KORDEGARDY — KURTA / LASKA
    - WIGA-WARA Z KORDEGARDY — SMOK Z KORDEGARDY / WIGA
  - CERTA Z MELNA
    - KROKUS Z KORDEGARDY — SMOK Z KORDEGARDY / DIUNA Z BABIEJ WSI
    - ERGA Z BABIEJ WSI — CZAR / BAJDA Z BABIEJ WSI
- DUMKA Z KORDEGARDY
  - KOMPAN Z KORDEGARDY
    03-09-1967 M
    - IN.PL.CH DOMAN Z KORDEGARDY — LIDER Z KORDEGARDY / CERTA Z MELNA
    - LONKA Z KORDEGARDY — ARAK-GREPS Z KORDEGARDY / ISIA Z KORDEGARDY
  - DRUMLA Z KORDEGARDY
    - GRZMOT Z KORDEGARDY — IN.PL.CH DOMAN Z KORDEGARDY / HAJDA Z KORDEGARDY
    - BEZA Z LAGIEWNICKIEGO BORU — IN.PL.CH AMOK MONIEK / POL.CH. SZELMA Z KORDEGARDY

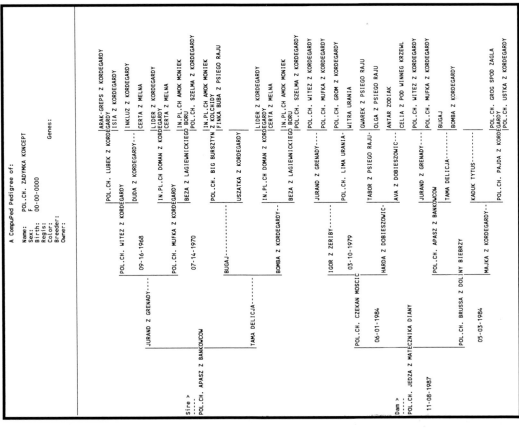

A CompuPed Pedigree of:

```
Name:    POL.CH. WITEZ Z KORDEGARDY
Sex:     M
Birth:   09-16-1968
Regis:
Color:                            Genes:
Breeder:
Owner:
```

```
                                                                          KUSY
                                                        SZLEM Z BABIEJ WSI-|
                                                        |                 BAJDA Z BABIEJ WSI
                                          DUKAT Z BABIEJ WSI-|
                                          |             BAJDA Z BABIEJ WSI-|BIES
                                          |                               BYSTRA
                           ARAK-GREPS Z KORDEGARDY-|
                           |              |                 KURTA
                           |              |       SMOK Z KORDEGARDY--|
                           |              |       |                 LASKA
                           |              NIWA Z KORDEGARDY--|
                           |                      |         SZLEM Z BABIEJ WSI
                           |                      DIUNA Z BABIEJ WSI-|
                           |                                        BAJDA Z BABIEJ WSI
Sire >                     |
-----                      |
POL.CH. LUBEK Z KORDEGARDY-|
                           |                                        KURTA
                           |                            SMOK Z KORDEGARDY--|
                           |                            |                 LASKA
                           |              KROKUS Z KORDEGARDY-|
                           |              |             SZLEM Z BABIEJ WSI
                           |              |             DIUNA Z BABIEJ WSI-|
                           |              |                              BAJDA Z BABIEJ WSI
                           ISIA Z KORDEGARDY---|
                                          |                 KURTA
                                          |       SMOK Z KORDEGARDY--|
                                          |       |                 LASKA
                                          IWA Z KORDEGARDY---|
                                                  |         SMOK Z KORDEGARDY
                                                  KUMA Z KORDEGARDY--|
                                                                    DIUNA Z BABIEJ WSI


                                                        KURTA-----------
                                          SMOK Z KORDEGARDY--|
                                          |             LASKA-----------
                           INKLUZ Z KORDEGARDY-|
                           |              |                 KURTA
                           |              KUMA Z KORDEGARDY--|
                           |              |             SMOK Z KORDEGARDY
                           |              |             DIUNA Z BABIEJ WSI-|
                           |              |                              LASKA
Dam >                      |
-----                      |
DUDA Z KORDEGARDY--|
                           |                            SMOK Z KORDEGARDY
                           |              KROKUS Z KORDEGARDY-|
                           |              |             SZLEM Z BABIEJ WSI
                           |              |             DIUNA Z BABIEJ WSI-|
                           CERTA Z MELNA------|                          BAJDA Z BABIEJ WSI
                                          |       CZAR-------------
                                          ERGA Z BABIEJ WSI-|
                                                  |         BIES
                                                  BAJDA Z BABIEJ WSI-|
                                                                    BYSTRA
```

A CompuPed Pedigree of:

```
Name:    POL.CH. ZADYMKA KONCEPT
Sex:     F
Birth:   00-00-0000
Regis:
Color:                            Genes:
Breeder:
Owner:
```

```
                                                        ARAK-GREPS Z KORDEGARDY
                                          POL.CH. LUBEK Z KORDEGARDY-|
                                          |             ISIA Z KORDEGARDY
                           POL.CH. WITEZ Z KORDEGARDY-|
                           |              |                 INKLUZ Z KORDEGARDY
                           |              DUDA Z KORDEGARDY--|
                           |              09-16-1968        CERTA Z MELNA
                           |                                        LIDER Z KORDEGARDY
                           |                            1N.PL.CH DOMAN Z KORDEGARDY-|
            JURAND Z GRENADY----|                       |                 CERTA Z MELNA
            |              POL.CH. MUFKA Z KORDEGARDY-|
            |              07-14-1970        BEZA Z LAGIEWNICKIEGO BORU-|1N.PL.CH AMOK MONIEK
            |                                                          POL.CH. SZELMA Z KORDEGARDY
Sire >      |
-----       |
POL.CH. APASZ Z BANKOWCOW-|
            |                                        1N.PL.CH AMOK MONIEK
            |                           POL.CH. BIG BURSZTYN Z KOLCHIDY
            |              BUGAJ-------------|        FINKA BUBA Z PSIEGO RAJU
            |              |              USZATKA Z KORDEGARDY
            TAMA DELICJA-------|
                           |                                        LIDER Z KORDEGARDY
                           |              1N.PL.CH DOMAN Z KORDEGARDY-|
                           BOMBA Z KORDEGARDY--|                     CERTA Z MELNA
                                          |             1N.PL.CH AMOK MONIEK
                                          BEZA Z LAGIEWNICKIEGO BORU-|
                                                        POL.CH. SZELMA Z KORDEGARDY


                                                        POL.CH. WITEZ Z KORDEGARDY
                                          JURAND Z GRENADY----|
                                          |             POL.CH. MUFKA Z KORDEGARDY
                           IGOR Z ZERIBY------|
                           |              |                 POL.CH. GROM Z KORDEGARDY
                           |              POL.CH. LIMA URANIA-|
                           |              03-10-1979        WITRA URANIA
            POL.CH. CZEKAN MOSCIC-|                                  GWAREK Z PSIEGO RAJU
            |              |                           TABOR Z PSIEGO RAJU-|
            |              06-01-1984                  |                 OLGA Z PSIEGO RAJU
            |              HARDA Z DOBIESZOWIC-|
            |                                |                 ANTAR ZODIAK
            |                                AVA Z DOBIESZOWIC-|
            |                                          CELIA Z POD WINNEG KRZEWL
Dam >       |
-----       |
POL.CH. JEDZA Z MATECZNIKA DIANY-|
            |                                        POL.CH. WITEZ Z KORDEGARDY
            |                           JURAND Z GRENADY----|
            |                           |             POL.CH. MUFKA Z KORDEGARDY
            |              POL.CH. APASZ Z BANKOWCOW-|
            |              |              |                 BUGAJ
            |              |              TAMA DELICJA------|
            |              |                                BOMBA Z KORDEGARDY
            POL.CH. BRUSSA Z DOLINY BIEBRZY-|
                           |              KADUK TYTUS----------
                           11-08-1987     |
                           05-03-1984     |                 POL.CH. GROG SPOD ZAGLA
                                          MAJKA Z KORDEGARDY--|
                                          |             POL.CH. PAJDA Z KORDEGARDY
                                                        POL.CH. USTKA Z KORDEGARDY
```

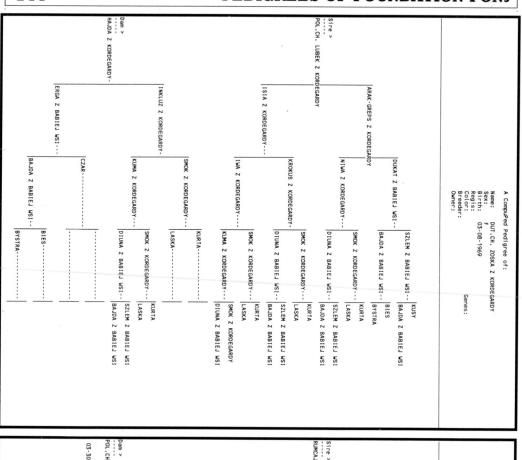

A CompuPed Pedigree of:

Name: DUT.CH. ZOSKA Z KORDEGARDY
Sex: F
Birth: 03-08-1969
Regis:
Color:
Breeder:
Owner:

Genes:

```
Sire >
POL.CH. LUBEK Z KORDEGARDY-
    │
    ├─ ARAK-GREPS Z KORDEGARDY-
    │       │
    │       ├─ DUKAT Z BABIEJ WSI--
    │       │       ├─ SZLEM Z BABIEJ WSI--
    │       │       │       ├─ KUSY
    │       │       │       └─ BAJDA Z BABIEJ WSI
    │       │       └─ BAJDA Z BABIEJ WSI--
    │       │               ├─ BIES
    │       │               └─ BYSTRA
    │       └─ NIWA Z KORDEGARDY---
    │               ├─ SMOK Z KORDEGARDY---
    │               │       ├─ KURTA
    │               │       └─ LASKA
    │               └─ DIUNA Z BABIEJ WSI--
    │                       ├─ SZLEM Z BABIEJ WSI
    │                       └─ BAJDA Z BABIEJ WSI
    └─ ISIA Z KORDEGARDY---
            │
            ├─ KROKUS Z KORDEGARDY---
            │       ├─ SMOK Z KORDEGARDY---
            │       │       ├─ KURTA
            │       │       └─ LASKA
            │       └─ DIUNA Z BABIEJ WSI--
            │               ├─ SZLEM Z BABIEJ WSI
            │               └─ BAJDA Z BABIEJ WSI
            └─ IWA Z KORDEGARDY---
                    ├─ SMOK Z KORDEGARDY---
                    │       ├─ KURTA
                    │       └─ LASKA
                    └─ KUMA Z KORDEGARDY---
                            ├─ SMOK Z KORDEGARDY
                            └─ DIUNA Z BABIEJ WSI

Dam >
HAJDA Z KORDEGARDY-
    │
    ├─ INKLUZ Z KORDEGARDY-
    │       │
    │       ├─ SMOK Z KORDEGARDY---
    │       │       ├─ KURTA----
    │       │       └─ LASKA----
    │       └─ KUMA Z KORDEGARDY---
    │               ├─ SMOK Z KORDEGARDY---
    │               └─ DIUNA Z BABIEJ WSI--
    │                       ├─ SZLEM Z BABIEJ WSI
    │                       └─ BAJDA Z BABIEJ WSI
    └─ ERGA Z BABIEJ WSI---
            │
            ├─ CZAR--
            │       ├─ KURTA----
            │       └─ LASKA----
            └─ BAJDA Z BABIEJ WSI---
                    ├─ BIES----
                    └─ BYSTRA----
```

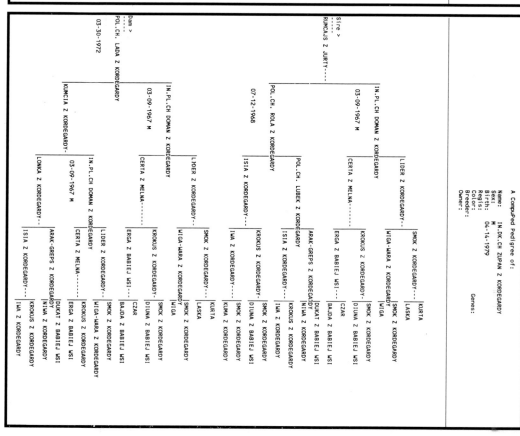

A CompuPed Pedigree of:

Name: IN.DK.CH ZUPAN Z KORDEGARDY
Sex: M
Birth: 04-14-1979
Regis:
Color:
Breeder:
Owner:

Genes:

```
Sire >
RUMCAJS Z JURTY----
    │
    ├─ IN.PL.CH DOMAN Z KORDEGARDY
    │   03-09-1967 M
    │       │
    │       ├─ LIDER Z KORDEGARDY-
    │       │       ├─ SMOK Z KORDEGARDY---
    │       │       │       ├─ KURTA
    │       │       │       └─ LASKA
    │       │       └─ WIGA-WARA Z KORDEGARDY---
    │       │               ├─ SMOK Z KORDEGARDY
    │       │               └─ WIGA
    │       └─ CERTA Z MELNA-------
    │               ├─ KROKUS Z KORDEGARDY---
    │               │       ├─ SMOK Z KORDEGARDY
    │               │       └─ DIUNA Z BABIEJ WSI
    │               └─ ERGA Z BABIEJ WSI---
    │                       ├─ CZAR
    │                       └─ BAJDA Z BABIEJ WSI
    └─ POL.CH. ROLA Z KORDEGARDY
        07-12-1968
            │
            ├─ POL.CH. LUBEK Z KORDEGARDY---
            │       ├─ ARAK-GREPS Z KORDEGARDY
            │       │       ├─ DUKAT Z BABIEJ WSI
            │       │       └─ NIWA Z KORDEGARDY
            │       └─ ISIA Z KORDEGARDY---
            │               ├─ KROKUS Z KORDEGARDY
            │               └─ IWA Z KORDEGARDY
            └─ ISIA Z KORDEGARDY---
                    ├─ KROKUS Z KORDEGARDY---
                    │       ├─ SMOK Z KORDEGARDY
                    │       └─ DIUNA Z BABIEJ WSI
                    └─ IWA Z KORDEGARDY---
                            ├─ SMOK Z KORDEGARDY
                            └─ KUMA Z KORDEGARDY

Dam >
POL.CH. LADA Z KORDEGARDY
03-30-1972
    │
    ├─ IN.PL.CH DOMAN Z KORDEGARDY
    │   03-09-1967 M
    │       │
    │       ├─ LIDER Z KORDEGARDY-
    │       │       ├─ SMOK Z KORDEGARDY---
    │       │       │       ├─ KURTA
    │       │       │       └─ LASKA
    │       │       └─ WIGA-WARA Z KORDEGARDY---
    │       │               ├─ SMOK Z KORDEGARDY
    │       │               └─ WIGA
    │       └─ CERTA Z MELNA------
    │               ├─ KROKUS Z KORDEGARDY---
    │               │       ├─ SMOK Z KORDEGARDY
    │               │       └─ DIUNA Z BABIEJ WSI
    │               └─ ERGA Z BABIEJ WSI---
    │                       ├─ CZAR
    │                       └─ BAJDA Z BABIEJ WSI
    └─ KUMCIA Z KORDEGARDY-
        03-09-1967 M
            │
            ├─ IN.PL.CH DOMAN Z KORDEGARDY---
            │       ├─ LIDER Z KORDEGARDY---
            │       │       ├─ SMOK Z KORDEGARDY
            │       │       └─ WIGA-WARA Z KORDEGARDY
            │       └─ CERTA Z MELNA---
            │               ├─ KROKUS Z KORDEGARDY
            │               └─ ERGA Z BABIEJ WSI
            └─ LONKA Z KORDEGARDY---
                    ├─ ARAK-GREPS Z KORDEGARDY---
                    │       ├─ DUKAT Z BABIEJ WSI
                    │       └─ NIWA Z KORDEGARDY
                    └─ ISIA Z KORDEGARDY---
                            ├─ KROKUS Z KORDEGARDY
                            └─ IWA Z KORDEGARDY
```

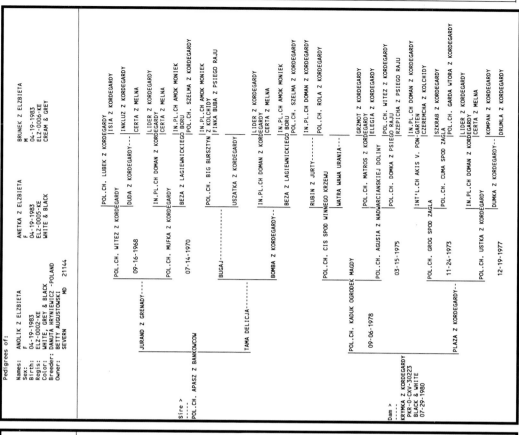

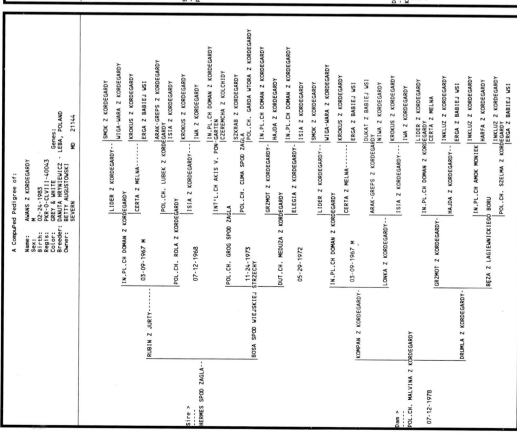

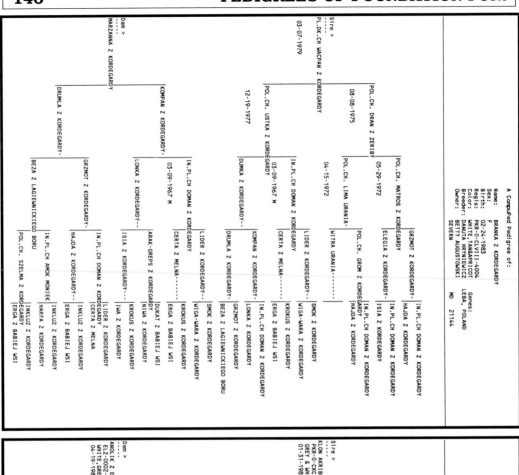

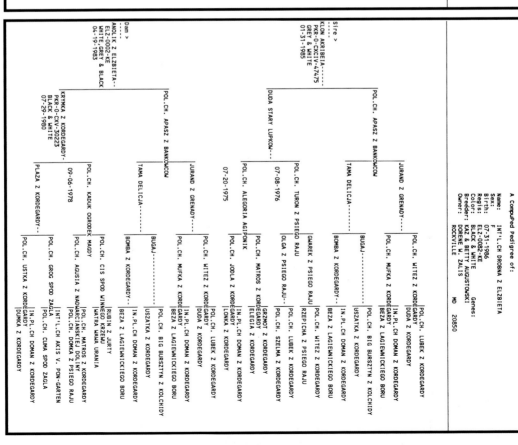

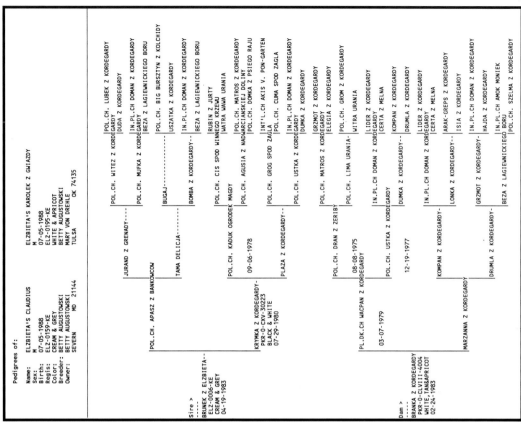

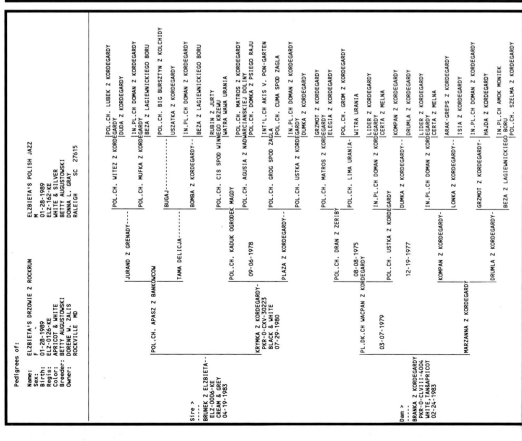

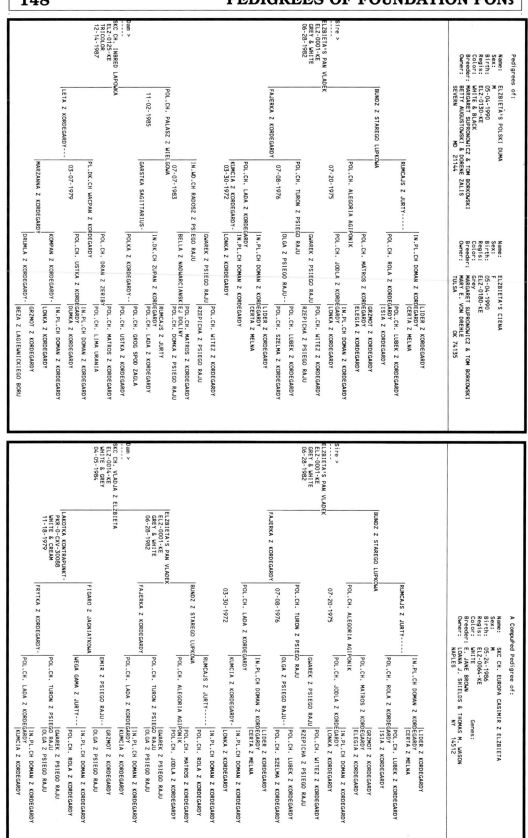

Pedigrees of:

Name: ELZBIETA'S POLSKI DUMA
Sex: M
Birth: 05-04-1990
Regis: ELZ-0130-KE
Color: WHITE & BLACK
Breeder: MARGARET SUPRONOWICZ & TOM BORKOWSKI
Owner: BETTY AUGUSTOWSKI & DORENE ZALIS
SEVERN MD 21144

Sire > ELZBIETA'S PAN VLADEK — ELZ-0001-KE — GREY & WHITE — 06-28-1982
- BUNDZ Z STAREGO LUPKOWA
  - POL.CH. ALEGORIA AGIPONIK — 07-20-1975
    - POL.CH. MATROS Z KORDEGARDY
      - GRZMOT Z KORDEGARDY
      - ELEGIA Z KORDEGARDY
    - IN.PL.CH DOMAN Z KORDEGARDY
      - LONKA Z KORDEGARDY
  - RUMCAJS Z JURTY
    - IN.PL.CH DOMAN Z KORDEGARDY
      - LIDER Z KORDEGARDY
      - CERTA Z MELNA
    - POL.CH. ROLA Z KORDEGARDY
      - POL.CH. LUBEK Z KORDEGARDY
      - ISIA Z KORDEGARDY
- FAJERKA Z KORDEGARDY — 07-08-1976
  - POL.CH. TURON Z PSIEGO RAJU
    - GWAREK Z PSIEGO RAJU
      - POL.CH. WITEZ Z KORDEGARDY
      - RZEPICHA Z PSIEGO RAJU
    - OLGA Z PSIEGO RAJU
      - POL.CH. LUBEK Z KORDEGARDY
      - POL.CH. SZELMA Z KORDEGARDY
  - KUMCIA Z KORDEGARDY — 03-30-1972
    - IN.PL.CH DOMAN Z KORDEGARDY
      - LIDER Z KORDEGARDY
      - CERTA Z MELNA
    - LONKA Z KORDEGARDY

Dam > SKC CH. INBRED LAPONKA — ELZ-0125-KE — TRICOLOR — 12-14-1987
- POL.CH. PALASZ Z WIELGOWA — 07-07-1983
  - IN.MD.CH RADOSZ Z PSIEGO RAJU
    - GWAREK Z PSIEGO RAJU
      - RZEPICHA Z PSIEGO RAJU
    - BELLA Z NADMARCIANSKIEJ DOLINY
      - POL.CH. MATROS Z KORDEGARDY
      - POL.CH. DOMKA Z PSIEGO RAJU
  - GARSTKA SAGITTARIUS — 11-02-1985
    - IN.DK.CH ZUPAN Z KORDEGARDY
      - RUMCAJS Z JURTY
      - POL.CH. LADA Z KORDEGARDY
    - POLKA Z KORDEGARDY
      - POL.CH. GROG SPOD ZAGLA
      - POL.CH. USTKA Z KORDEGARDY
- LETA Z KORDEGARDY — 03-07-1979
  - PL.DK.CH WACPAN Z KORDEGARDY
    - POL.CH. DRAN Z ZERIB
      - POL.CH. DOMAN Z KORDEGARDY
      - POL.CH. LIMA URANIA
    - POL.CH. USTKA Z KORDEGARDY
      - IN.PL.CH DOMAN Z KORDEGARDY
      - DUMKA Z KORDEGARDY
  - MARZANNA Z KORDEGARDY
    - KOMPAN Z KORDEGARDY
      - IN.PL.CH DOMAN Z KORDEGARDY
      - LONKA Z KORDEGARDY
    - DRUMLA Z KORDEGARDY
      - GRZMOT Z KORDEGARDY
      - BEZA Z LAGIEWNICKIEGO BORU

Name: ELZBIETA'S CIENA
Sex: F
Birth: 05-04-1990
Regis: ELZ-0180-KE
Color: GREY & WHITE
Breeder: MARGARET SUPRONOWICZ & TOM BORKOWSKI
Owner: MARY E. VON DREHLE
TULSA OK 74135

Sire > ELZBIETA'S PAN VLADEK — ELZ-0001-KE — GREY & WHITE — 06-28-1982
- BUNDZ Z STAREGO LUPKOWA
  - POL.CH. ALEGORIA AGIPONIK — 07-20-1975
    - POL.CH. MATROS Z KORDEGARDY
      - GRZMOT Z KORDEGARDY
      - ELEGIA Z KORDEGARDY
    - IN.PL.CH DOMAN Z KORDEGARDY
      - LONKA Z KORDEGARDY
  - RUMCAJS Z JURTY
    - IN.PL.CH DOMAN Z KORDEGARDY
      - LIDER Z KORDEGARDY
      - CERTA Z MELNA
    - POL.CH. ROLA Z KORDEGARDY
      - POL.CH. LUBEK Z KORDEGARDY
      - ISIA Z KORDEGARDY
- FAJERKA Z KORDEGARDY — 07-08-1976
  - POL.CH. TURON Z PSIEGO RAJU
    - GWAREK Z PSIEGO RAJU
      - POL.CH. WITEZ Z KORDEGARDY
      - RZEPICHA Z PSIEGO RAJU
    - OLGA Z PSIEGO RAJU
      - POL.CH. LUBEK Z KORDEGARDY
      - POL.CH. SZELMA Z KORDEGARDY
  - KUMCIA Z KORDEGARDY — 03-30-1972
    - IN.PL.CH DOMAN Z KORDEGARDY
    - LONKA Z KORDEGARDY

Dam > SKC CH. VLADJA Z ELZBIETA — ELZ-0014-KE — WHITE & GREY — 04-05-1984
- ELZBIETA'S PAN VLADEK — ELZ-0001-KE — GREY & WHITE — 06-28-1982
  - BUNDZ Z STAREGO LUPKOWA
    - POL.CH. ALEGORIA AGIPONIK — 07-20-1975
      - POL.CH. MATROS Z KORDEGARDY
      - IN.PL.CH DOMAN Z KORDEGARDY
    - RUMCAJS Z JURTY
      - IN.PL.CH DOMAN Z KORDEGARDY
      - POL.CH. ROLA Z KORDEGARDY
  - FAJERKA Z KORDEGARDY — 07-08-1976
    - POL.CH. TURON Z PSIEGO RAJU
      - GWAREK Z PSIEGO RAJU
      - OLGA Z PSIEGO RAJU
    - KUMCIA Z KORDEGARDY — 03-30-1972
      - IN.PL.CH DOMAN Z KORDEGARDY
      - LONKA Z KORDEGARDY
- LAKOTKA KONTRAPUNKT — PKR-0-CXV-30088 — WHITE & CREAM — 11-18-1979
  - FIGARO Z JAGNIATKOWA
    - EMIR Z PSIEGO RAJU
      - GRZMOT Z KORDEGARDY
      - POL.CH. ROLA Z KORDEGARDY
    - WEGA GAMA Z JURTY
      - IN.PL.CH DOMAN Z KORDEGARDY
      - POL.CH. TURON Z PSIEGO RAJU
  - FRYTKA Z KORDEGARDY
    - POL.CH. TURON Z PSIEGO RAJU
      - GWAREK Z PSIEGO RAJU
      - OLGA Z PSIEGO RAJU
    - IN.PL.CH DOMAN Z KORDEGARDY
      - POL.CH. LADA Z KORDEGARDY
      - KUMCIA Z KORDEGARDY

A CompuPed Pedigree of:

Name: SKC CH. EUROPA CASIMIR Z ELZBIETA
Sex: M
Birth: 05-24-1986
Regis: ELZ-0064-KE
Color: WHITE
Breeder: E. JANE BROWN
Owner: DIANA J. SHIELDS & THOMAS M. MASON
NAPLES NY 14512
Genes:

Sire > ELZBIETA'S PAN VLADEK — ELZ-0001-KE — GREY & WHITE — 06-28-1982
- BUNDZ Z STAREGO LUPKOWA
  - POL.CH. ALEGORIA AGIPONIK — 07-20-1975
    - POL.CH. MATROS Z KORDEGARDY
      - GRZMOT Z KORDEGARDY
      - ELEGIA Z KORDEGARDY
    - IN.PL.CH DOMAN Z KORDEGARDY
      - LONKA Z KORDEGARDY
  - RUMCAJS Z JURTY
    - IN.PL.CH DOMAN Z KORDEGARDY
      - LIDER Z KORDEGARDY
      - CERTA Z MELNA
    - POL.CH. ROLA Z KORDEGARDY
      - POL.CH. LUBEK Z KORDEGARDY
      - ISIA Z KORDEGARDY
- FAJERKA Z KORDEGARDY — 07-08-1976
  - POL.CH. TURON Z PSIEGO RAJU
    - GWAREK Z PSIEGO RAJU
      - POL.CH. WITEZ Z KORDEGARDY
      - RZEPICHA Z PSIEGO RAJU
    - OLGA Z PSIEGO RAJU
      - POL.CH. LUBEK Z KORDEGARDY
      - POL.CH. SZELMA Z KORDEGARDY
  - KUMCIA Z KORDEGARDY — 03-30-1972
    - IN.PL.CH DOMAN Z KORDEGARDY
      - POL.CH. LADA Z KORDEGARDY
      - KUMCIA Z KORDEGARDY

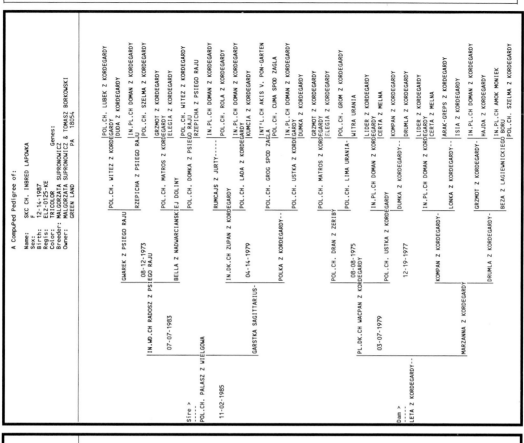

A CompuPed Pedigree of:

Name: KLON AKRIBEIA
Sex: M
Birth: 01-31-1985
Regis: KKR-0-CXCIY-47475
Color: GREY & WHITE   Genes:
Breeder: BOGUSLAWA PATRZYKONT - POZNAN, POLAND
Owner: BETTY AUGUSTOWSKI
SEVERN   MD   21144

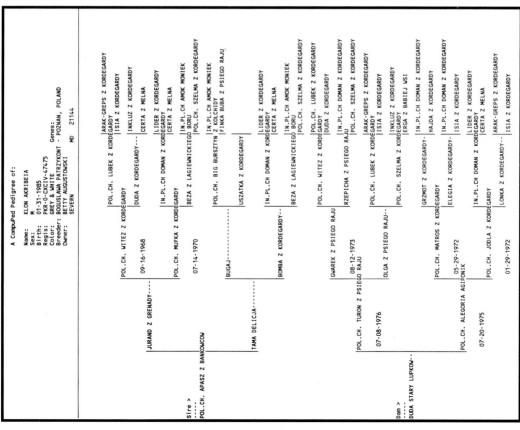

A CompuPed Pedigree of:

Name: SKC CH. INBRED LAPOKKA
Sex: F
Birth: 12-14-1987
Regis: ELZ-0125-KE
Color: TRICOLOR   Genes:
Breeder: MALGORZATA SUPRONOWICZ
Owner: MALGORZATA SUPRONOWICZ & TOMASZ BORKOWSKI
GREEN LAND   PA   18054

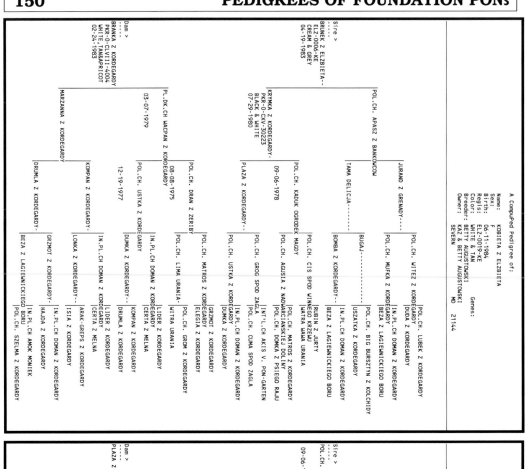

A CompuPed Pedigree of:

Name: KOBIETA Z ELZBIETA
Sex: F
Birth: 06-11-1984
Regis: ELZ-0019-KE
Color: WHITE & TAN
Breeder: BETTY AUGUSTOWSKI
Owner: KAZ & BETTY AUGUSTOWSKI
SEVERN MD
Genes: 21144

Sire > BRUNEK Z ELZBIETA — ELZ-0006-KE, CREAM & GREY, 04-19-1983

- POL.CH. APASZ Z BANKOWCOW
  - JURAND Z GRENADY
    - POL.CH. WITEZ Z KORDEGARDY
      - POL.CH. LUBEK Z KORDEGARDY
      - DUDA Z KORDEGARDY
    - POL.CH. MUFKA Z KORDEGARDY
      - IN.PL.CH DOMAN Z KORDEGARDY
      - BEZA Z LAGIEWNICKIEGO BORU
  - TAMA DELICJA
    - BUGAJ
      - POL.CH. BIG BURSZTYN Z KOLCHIDY
      - USZATKA Z KORDEGARDY
    - BOMBA Z KORDEGARDY
      - IN.PL.CH DOMAN Z KORDEGARDY
      - BEZA Z LAGIEWNICKIEGO BORU
- KRYMKA Z KORDEGARDY — PKR-0-CXV-30223, BLACK & WHITE, 07-29-1980
  - PL.DK.CH WACPAN Z KORDEGARDY — 03-07-1979
    - POL.CH. KADUK OGRODEK MAGDY — 08-08-1975
      - POL.CH. CIS SPOD WINNEGO KRZEWU
        - RUBIN Z JURTY
        - WATRA WAWA URANIA
      - POL.CH. MATROS Z KORDEGARDY
        - GRZMOT Z KORDEGARDY
        - ELEGIA Z KORDEGARDY
    - POL.CH. USTKA Z KORDEGARDY — 12-19-1977
      - POL.CH. DRAN Z ZERIBY
        - POL.CH. LIMA URANIA
          - WITRA URANIA
        - POL.CH. GROM Z KORDEGARDY
      - POL.CH. AGUSIA Z NADWARCIANSKIEJ DOLINY
        - INT'L.CH AKIS V. PON-GARTEN
        - POL.CH. DOMKA Z PSIEGO RAJU
  - PLAZA Z KORDEGARDY — 09-06-1978
    - POL.CH. GROG SPOD ZAGLA
      - POL.CH. CUMA SPOD ZAGLA
      - IN.PL.CH DOMAN Z KORDEGARDY
    - POL.CH. USTKA Z KORDEGARDY
      - IN.PL.CH DOMAN Z KORDEGARDY
      - DUMKA Z KORDEGARDY

Dam > BRANKA Z KORDEGARDY — PKR-0-CLVIII-4004, WHITE, TAN & APRICOT, 02-24-1983

- MARZANNA Z KORDEGARDY
  - KOMPAN Z KORDEGARDY — 12-19-1977
    - IN.PL.CH DOMAN Z KORDEGARDY
      - LIDER Z KORDEGARDY
      - CERTA Z MELNA
    - LONKA Z KORDEGARDY
      - ISIA Z KORDEGARDY
      - ARAK-GREPS Z KORDEGARDY
  - DRUMLA Z KORDEGARDY
    - GRZMOT Z KORDEGARDY
      - IN.PL.CH DOMAN Z KORDEGARDY
      - BEZA Z LAGIEWNICKIEGO BORU
    - HAJDA Z KORDEGARDY
      - IN.PL.CH DOMAN Z KORDEGARDY
      - POL.CH. SZELMA Z KORDEGARDY

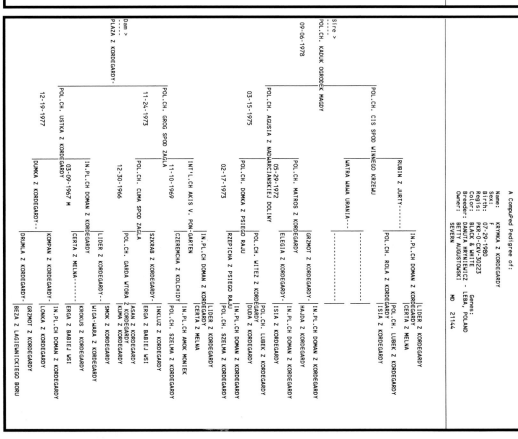

A CompuPed Pedigree of:

Name: KRYMKA Z KORDEGARDY
Sex: F
Birth: 07-29-1980
Regis: PKR-0-CXV-30223
Color: BLACK & WHITE
Breeder: DANUTA HRYNIEWICZ - LEBA, POLAND
Owner: BETTY AUGUSTOWSKI
SEVERN MD
Genes: 21144

Sire > POL.CH. KADUK OGRODEK MAGDY — 09-06-1978

- POL.CH. CIS SPOD WINNEGO KRZEWU
  - RUBIN Z JURTY
    - IN.PL.CH DOMAN Z KORDEGARDY
      - LIDER Z KORDEGARDY
      - CERTA Z MELNA
    - POL.CH. ROLA Z KORDEGARDY
      - POL.CH. LUBEK Z KORDEGARDY
      - ISIA Z KORDEGARDY
  - WATRA WAWA URANIA
    - POL.CH. AGUSIA Z NADWARCIANSKIEJ DOLINY — 03-15-1975
      - INT'L.CH AKIS V. PON-GARTEN — 02-17-1973
      - POL.CH. DOMKA Z PSIEGO RAJU
        - RZEPICHA Z PSIEGO RAJU
        - CZEREMCHA Z KOLCHIDY
- POL.CH. MATROS Z KORDEGARDY — 05-29-1972
  - GRZMOT Z KORDEGARDY — 11-10-1969
    - IN.PL.CH DOMAN Z KORDEGARDY
    - HAJDA Z KORDEGARDY
      - POL.CH. SZELMA Z KORDEGARDY
      - POL.CH. AMOK MONIEK
  - ELEGIA Z KORDEGARDY
    - IN.PL.CH DOMAN Z KORDEGARDY
    - ISIA Z KORDEGARDY

Dam > PLAZA Z KORDEGARDY — 09-06-1978

- POL.CH. GROG SPOD ZAGLA — 11-10-1969
  - POL.CH. CUMA SPOD ZAGLA — 12-30-1966
    - SZKRAB Z KORDEGARDY
      - INKLUZ Z KORDEGARDY
      - ERGA Z BABIEJ WSI
    - POL.CH. GARDA WTORA Z KORDEGARDY
      - ASAN Z KORDEGARDY
      - KUMA Z KORDEGARDY
  - IN.PL.CH DOMAN Z KORDEGARDY
    - LIDER Z KORDEGARDY
    - CERTA Z MELNA
- POL.CH. USTKA Z KORDEGARDY — 12-19-1977
  - IN.PL.CH DOMAN Z KORDEGARDY — 03-09-1967 M
    - KOMPAN Z KORDEGARDY
      - SMOK Z KORDEGARDY
      - WIGA-WARA Z KORDEGARDY
    - CERTA Z MELNA
      - KROKUS Z KORDEGARDY
      - ERGA Z BABIEJ WSI
  - DUMKA Z KORDEGARDY
    - IN.PL.CH DOMAN Z KORDEGARDY
      - LONKA Z KORDEGARDY
      - GRZMOT Z KORDEGARDY
    - DRUMLA Z KORDEGARDY
      - GRZMOT Z KORDEGARDY
      - BEZA Z LAGIEWNICKIEGO BORU

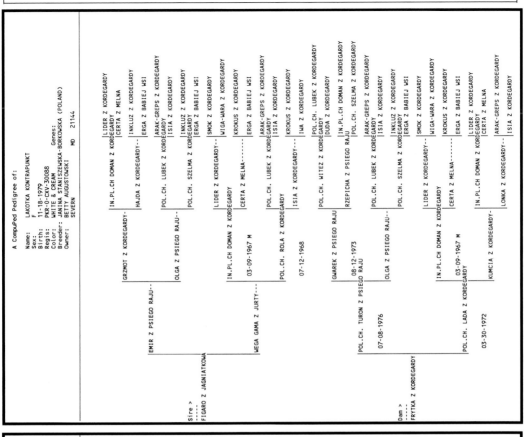

A CompuPed Pedigree of:

Name: LAKOTKA KONTRAPUNKT
Sex: F
Birth: 11-18-1979
Regis: PKR-O-CXV-30088
Color: WHITE & CREAM
Breeder: JANINA STANISZEWSKA-BORKOWSKA (POLAND)
Owner: BETTY AUGUSTOWSKI
SEVERN   MD   21144   Genes:

```
Sire >
-----
FIGARO Z JAGNIATKOWA

  EMIR Z PSIEGO RAJU--
    GRZMOT Z KORDEGARDY-
      IN.PL.CH DOMAN Z KORDEGARDY-
        LIDER Z KORDEGARDY
        CERTA Z MELNA
      HAJDA Z KORDEGARDY-
        INKLUZ Z KORDEGARDY
        ERGA Z BABIEJ WSI
    OLGA Z PSIEGO RAJU--
      POL.CH. LUBEK Z KORDEGARDY
        ARAK-GREPS Z KORDEGARDY
        ISIA Z KORDEGARDY
      POL.CH. SZELMA Z KORDEGARDY
        INKLUZ Z KORDEGARDY
        ERGA Z BABIEJ WSI

  WEGA GAMA Z JURTY---
    03-09-1967 M
      IN.PL.CH DOMAN Z KORDEGARDY
        LIDER Z KORDEGARDY
        CERTA Z MELNA------
          SMOK Z KORDEGARDY
          WIGA-WARA Z KORDEGARDY
            KROKUS Z KORDEGARDY
            ERGA Z BABIEJ WSI
      POL.CH. ROLA Z KORDEGARDY
        POL.CH. LUBEK Z KORDEGARDY
          ARAK-GREPS Z KORDEGARDY
          ISIA Z KORDEGARDY
        ISIA Z KORDEGARDY
          KROKUS Z KORDEGARDY
          IWA Z KORDEGARDY
      07-12-1968
```

```
Dam >
-----
FRYTKA Z KORDEGARDY

  POL.CH. TURON Z PSIEGO RAJU
    GWAREK Z PSIEGO RAJU
      POL.CH. WITEZ Z KORDEGARDY
        POL.CH. LUBEK Z KORDEGARDY
        DUDA Z KORDEGARDY
      RZEPICHA Z PSIEGO RAJU
        IN.PL.CH DOMAN Z KORDEGARDY
        POL.CH. SZELMA Z KORDEGARDY
    08-12-1973
      POL.CH. LUBEK Z KORDEGARDY
        ARAK-GREPS Z KORDEGARDY
        ISIA Z KORDEGARDY
      POL.CH. SZELMA Z KORDEGARDY
        INKLUZ Z KORDEGARDY
        ERGA Z BABIEJ WSI
    07-08-1976
      OLGA Z PSIEGO RAJU--
        SMOK Z KORDEGARDY
        WIGA-WARA Z KORDEGARDY
          KROKUS Z KORDEGARDY
          ERGA Z BABIEJ WSI

  POL.CH. LADA Z KORDEGARDY
    IN.PL.CH DOMAN Z KORDEGARDY
      LIDER Z KORDEGARDY
      CERTA Z MELNA------
    03-09-1967 M
      LIDER Z KORDEGARDY
      CERTA Z MELNA
    KUMCIA Z KORDEGARDY
      IN.PL.CH DOMAN Z KORDEGARDY
        ARAK-GREPS Z KORDEGARDY
        ISIA Z KORDEGARDY
      LONKA Z KORDEGARDY
    03-30-1972
```

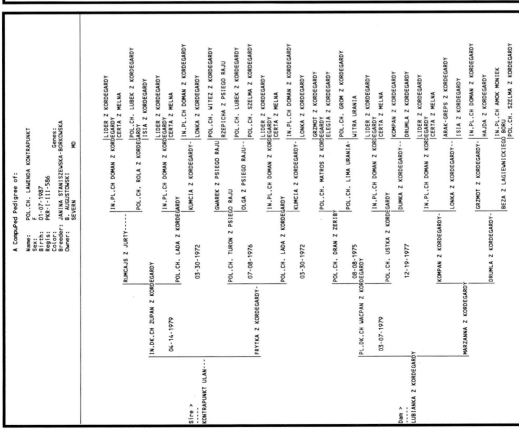

A CompuPed Pedigree of:

Name: POL.CH. LAWENDA KONTRAPUNKT
Sex: F
Birth: 01-07-1987
Regis: PKR-1-III-586
Color:
Breeder: JANINA STANISZEWSKA-BORKOWSKA
Owner: B. AUGUSTOWSKI
SEVERN   MD   Genes:

```
Sire >
-----
KONTRAPUNKT ULAN---

  IN.DK.CH ZUPAN Z KORDEGARDY
    RUMCAJS Z JURTY-----
      IN.PL.CH DOMAN Z KORDEGARDY-
        LIDER Z KORDEGARDY
        CERTA Z MELNA
      POL.CH. ROLA Z KORDEGARDY-
        POL.CH. LUBEK Z KORDEGARDY
        ISIA Z KORDEGARDY
    04-14-1979
      POL.CH. LADA Z KORDEGARDY
        IN.PL.CH DOMAN Z KORDEGARDY
          LIDER Z KORDEGARDY
          CERTA Z MELNA
        KUMCIA Z KORDEGARDY
          IN.PL.CH DOMAN Z KORDEGARDY
          LONKA Z KORDEGARDY
      03-30-1972

  FRYTKA Z KORDEGARDY-
    POL.CH. TURON Z PSIEGO RAJU
      GWAREK Z PSIEGO RAJU
        POL.CH. WITEZ Z KORDEGARDY
        RZEPICHA Z PSIEGO RAJU
      OLGA Z PSIEGO RAJU--
        POL.CH. LUBEK Z KORDEGARDY
        POL.CH. SZELMA Z KORDEGARDY
    07-08-1976
      POL.CH. LADA Z KORDEGARDY
        IN.PL.CH DOMAN Z KORDEGARDY
          LIDER Z KORDEGARDY
          CERTA Z MELNA
        KUMCIA Z KORDEGARDY-
          IN.PL.CH DOMAN Z KORDEGARDY
          LONKA Z KORDEGARDY
    03-30-1972
```

```
Dam >
-----
LUBIANKA Z KORDEGARDY

  PL.DK.CH WACPAN Z KORDEGARDY
    POL.CH. DRAN Z ZERIB'
      POL.CH. MATROS Z KORDEGARDY
        GRZMOT Z KORDEGARDY
        ELEGIA Z KORDEGARDY
      POL.CH. GROM Z KORDEGARDY
        POL.CH. LIMA URANIA-
        WITRA URANIA
    08-08-1975
      POL.CH. USTKA Z KORDEGARDY
        IN.PL.CH DOMAN Z KORDEGARDY
          LIDER Z KORDEGARDY
          CERTA Z MELNA
        KOMPAN Z KORDEGARDY
        DUMKA Z KORDEGARDY
          DRUMLA Z KORDEGARDY
    03-07-1979
    12-19-1977

  MARZANNA Z KORDEGARDY
    KOMPAN Z KORDEGARDY
      IN.PL.CH DOMAN Z KORDEGARDY
        LIDER Z KORDEGARDY
        CERTA Z MELNA
      LONKA Z KORDEGARDY-
        ARAK-GREPS Z KORDEGARDY
        ISIA Z KORDEGARDY
    GRZMOT Z KORDEGARDY-
      IN.PL.CH DOMAN Z KORDEGARDY
        HAJDA Z KORDEGARDY
      BEZA Z LAGIEWNICKIEGO BORU
        IN.PL.CH AMOK MONIEK
        POL.CH. SZELMA Z KORDEGARDY
    DRUMLA Z KORDEGARDY-
```

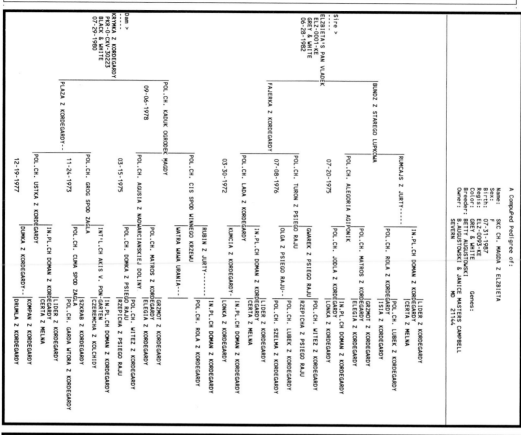

A CompuPed Pedigree of:

Name: SKC CH. MAGDA Z ELZBIETA
Sex: F
Birth: 07-31-1987
Regis: ELZ-0093-KE
Color: GREY & WHITE
Breeder: B. AUGUSTOWSKI
Owner: MARY KAZ & BETTY MASTERS CAMPBELL
SEVERN MD 21144
Genes:

Sire > ELZBIETA'S PAN VLADEK — ELZ-0001-KE — GREY & WHITE — 06-28-1982

- BUNDZ Z STAREGO LUPKOWA — 09-06-1978
  - RUMCAJS Z JURTY-----
    - IN.PL.CH DOMAN Z KORDEGARDY
      - LIDER Z KORDEGARDY
      - CERTA Z MELNA
    - POL.CH. ROLA Z KORDEGARDY
      - POL.CH. LUBEK Z KORDEGARDY
      - ISIA Z KORDEGARDY
  - POL.CH. ALEGORIA AGIPONIK — 07-20-1975
    - POL.CH. MATROS Z KORDEGARDY
      - GRZMOT Z KORDEGARDY
      - ELEGIA Z KORDEGARDY
    - POL.CH. JODLA Z KORDEGARDY
      - IN.PL.CH DOMAN Z KORDEGARDY
      - LONKA Z KORDEGARDY
- FAJERKA Z KORDEGARDY — 07-08-1976
  - POL.CH. TURON Z PSIEGO RAJU — 07-20-1975
    - GWAREK Z PSIEGO RAJU
      - POL.CH. WITEZ Z KORDEGARDY
      - RZEPICHA Z PSIEGO RAJU
    - OLGA Z PSIEGO RAJU--
      - POL.CH. LUBEK Z KORDEGARDY
      - POL.CH. SZELMA Z KORDEGARDY
  - POL.CH. LADA Z KORDEGARDY — 03-30-1972
    - IN.PL.CH DOMAN Z KORDEGARDY
      - LIDER Z KORDEGARDY
      - CERTA Z MELNA
    - KUMCIA Z KORDEGARDY
      - IN.PL.CH DOMAN Z KORDEGARDY
      - LONKA Z KORDEGARDY

Dam > KRYMKA Z KORDEGARDY — PKR-O-CXV-30223 — BLACK & WHITE — 07-29-1980

- POL.CH. KADUK OGRODEK MAGDY — 09-06-1978
  - POL.CH. CIS SPOD WINNEGO KRZEWU
    - RUBIN Z JURTY------
      - IN.PL.CH DOMAN Z KORDEGARDY
      - POL.CH. ROLA Z KORDEGARDY
    - WATRA WAWA URANIA---
  - POL.CH. AGUSTA Z NADWARCIANSKIEJ DOLINY — 03-15-1975
    - POL.CH. MATROS Z KORDEGARDY
      - GRZMOT Z KORDEGARDY
      - ELEGIA Z KORDEGARDY
    - POL.CH. DOMKA Z PSIEGO RAJU
      - INT'L.CH AKIS V. PON GARTEN
      - RZEPICHA Z PSIEGO RAJU
- PLAZA Z KORDEGARDY-- — 12-19-1977
  - POL.CH. GROG SPOD ZAGLA — 11-24-1973
    - INT'L.CH AKIS V. PON GARTEN
      - CZEREMCHA Z KOLCHIDY
    - POL.CH. CUMA SPOD ZAGLA
      - SZKRAB Z KORDEGARDY
      - POL.CH. GARDA WIORA Z KORDEGARDY
  - POL.CH. USTKA Z KORDEGARDY — 11-24-1977
    - IN.PL.CH DOMAN Z KORDEGARDY
      - LIDER Z KORDEGARDY
      - CERTA Z MELNA
    - DUMKA Z KORDEGARDY
      - KOMPAN Z KORDEGARDY
      - DRUMLA Z KORDEGARDY

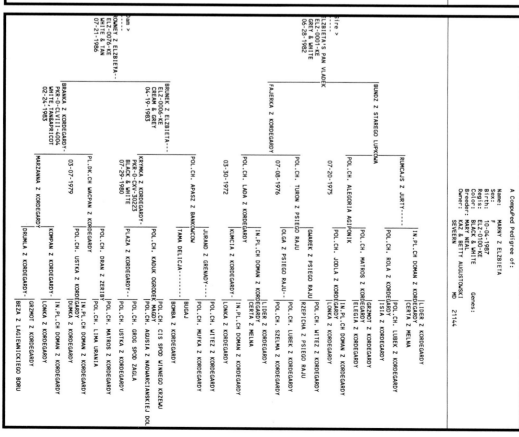

A CompuPed Pedigree of:

Name: MARNY Z ELZBIETA
Sex: F
Birth: 10-04-1987
Regis: ELZ-0100-KE
Color: BLACK & WHITE
Breeder: MARY NEAL
Owner: KAZ & BETTY AUGUSTOWSKI
SEVERN MD 21144
Genes:

Sire > ELZBIETA'S PAN VLADEK — ELZ-0001-KE — GREY & WHITE — 06-28-1982

- BUNDZ Z STAREGO LUPKOWA
  - RUMCAJS Z JURTY-----
    - IN.PL.CH DOMAN Z KORDEGARDY
      - LIDER Z KORDEGARDY
      - CERTA Z MELNA
    - POL.CH. ROLA Z KORDEGARDY
      - POL.CH. LUBEK Z KORDEGARDY
      - ISIA Z KORDEGARDY
  - POL.CH. ALEGORIA AGIPONIK — 07-20-1975
    - POL.CH. MATROS Z KORDEGARDY
      - GRZMOT Z KORDEGARDY
      - ELEGIA Z KORDEGARDY
    - POL.CH. JODLA Z KORDEGARDY
      - IN.PL.CH DOMAN Z KORDEGARDY
      - LONKA Z KORDEGARDY
- FAJERKA Z KORDEGARDY — 07-08-1976
  - POL.CH. TURON Z PSIEGO RAJU — 07-20-1975
    - GWAREK Z PSIEGO RAJU
      - POL.CH. WITEZ Z KORDEGARDY
      - RZEPICHA Z PSIEGO RAJU
    - OLGA Z PSIEGO RAJU--
      - POL.CH. LUBEK Z KORDEGARDY
      - POL.CH. SZELMA Z KORDEGARDY
  - POL.CH. LADA Z KORDEGARDY — 03-30-1972
    - IN.PL.CH DOMAN Z KORDEGARDY
      - LIDER Z KORDEGARDY
      - CERTA Z MELNA
    - KUMCIA Z KORDEGARDY
      - IN.PL.CH DOMAN Z KORDEGARDY
      - LONKA Z KORDEGARDY

Dam > RONNEY Z ELZBIETA-- — ELZ-0076-KE — WHITE & TAN — 07-21-1986

- BRUNEK Z ELZBIETA--- — ELZ-0006-KE — CREAM & GREY — 04-19-1983
  - POL.CH. KADUK OGRODEK MAGDY
    - POL.CH. CIS SPOD WINNEGO KRZEWU
      - JURAND Z GRENADY----
      - BOMBA Z KORDEGARDY
    - POL.CH. APASZ Z BANKOWCOW
      - TAMA DELICJA------
      - BUGAJ
  - KRYMKA Z KORDEGARDY- — PKR-O-CXV-30223 — BLACK & WHITE — 07-29-1980
    - POL.CH. KADUK OGRODEK MAGDY
      - POL.CH. KADUK OGRODEK MAGDY
      - POL.CH. AGUSTA Z NADWARCIANSKIEJ DOL
    - PLAZA Z KORDEGARDY
      - POL.CH. MATROS Z KORDEGARDY
      - DUMKA Z KORDEGARDY
- BRANKA Z KORDEGARDY- — PKR-O-CLVIII-4004 — WHITE,TAN&APRICOT — 02-24-1983
  - PL.DK.CH. MACPAN Z KORDEGARDY — 03-07-1979
    - POL.CH. DRAN Z ZERIBA
      - POL.CH. MATROS Z KORDEGARDY
      - POL.CH. USTKA Z KORDEGARDY
    - POL.CH. LIMA URANIA
      - IN.PL.CH DOMAN Z KORDEGARDY
      - LONKA Z KORDEGARDY
  - MARZANNA Z KORDEGARDY
    - KOMPAN Z KORDEGARDY-
      - GRZMOT Z KORDEGARDY
      - BEZA Z LAGIEWNICKIEGO BORU
    - DRUMLA Z KORDEGARDY-

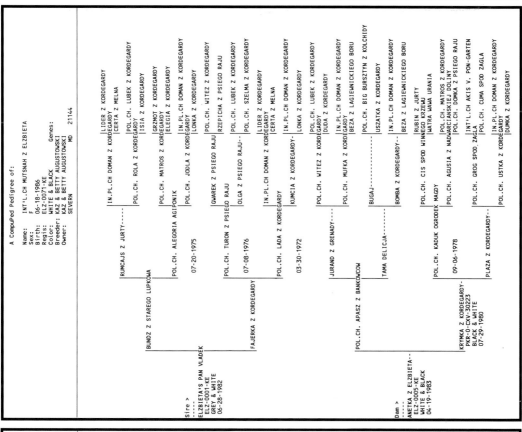

A CompuPed Pedigree of:

Name: INT'L.CH MUTSNAH Z ELZBIETA
Sex: F
Birth: 06-18-1986
Regis: ELZ-0071-KE
Color: WHITE & BLACK   Genes:
Breeder: KAZ & BETTY AUGUSTOWSKI
Owner: KAZ & BETTY AUGUSTOWSKI
         SEVERN   MD   21144

Sire >
ELZBIETA'S PAN VLADEK
ELZ-0001-KE
GREY & WHITE
06-28-1982

- BUNDZ Z STAREGO LUPKOWA
  - RUMCAJS Z JURTY
    - IN.PL.CH DOMAN Z KORDEGARDY
      - LIDER Z KORDEGARDY
      - CERTA Z MELNA
    - POL.CH. ROLA Z KORDEGARDY
      - POL.CH. LUBEK Z KORDEGARDY
      - ISIA Z KORDEGARDY
  - POL.CH. ALEGORIA AGIPONIK 07-20-1975
    - POL.CH. MATROS Z KORDEGARDY
      - GRZMOT Z KORDEGARDY
      - ELEGIA Z KORDEGARDY
    - POL.CH. JOOLA Z KORDEGARDY
      - IN.PL.CH DOMAN Z KORDEGARDY
      - LONKA Z KORDEGARDY
- FAJERKA Z KORDEGARDY
  - POL.CH. TURON Z PSIEGO RAJU 07-08-1976
    - GWAREK Z PSIEGO RAJU
      - POL.CH. WITEZ Z KORDEGARDY
      - RZEPICHA Z PSIEGO RAJU
    - OLGA Z PSIEGO RAJU
      - POL.CH. LUBEK Z KORDEGARDY
      - POL.CH. SZELMA Z KORDEGARDY
  - POL.CH. LADA Z KORDEGARDY 03-30-1972
    - IN.PL.CH DOMAN Z KORDEGARDY
      - LIDER Z KORDEGARDY
      - CERTA Z MELNA
    - KUMCIA Z KORDEGARDY
      - POL.CH. LUBEK Z KORDEGARDY
      - DUDA Z KORDEGARDY

Dam >
ANETKA Z ELZBIETA
ELZ-0005-KE
WHITE & BLACK
04-19-1983

- POL.CH. APASZ Z BANKOWCOW
  - JURAND Z GRENADY
    - POL.CH. WITEZ Z KORDEGARDY
      - IN.PL.CH DOMAN Z KORDEGARDY
      - BEZA Z LAGIEWNICKIEGO BORU
    - POL.CH. MUFKA Z KORDEGARDY
      - POL.CH. BIG BURSZTYN Z KOLCHIDY
      - USZATKA Z KORDEGARDY
  - TAMA DELICJA
    - BUGAJ
      - IN.PL.CH DOMAN Z KORDEGARDY
      - BEZA Z LAGIEWNICKIEGO BORU
    - BOMBA Z KORDEGARDY
- KRYMKA Z KORDEGARDY
  PKR-0-CXV-30223
  BLACK & WHITE
  07-29-1980
  - POL.CH. KADUK OGRODEK MAGDY 09-06-1978
    - POL.CH. CIS SPOD WINNEGO KRZEWU
      - RUBIN Z JURTY
      - WATRA WAWA URANIA
    - POL.CH. AGUSIA Z NADVARCIANSKIEJ DOLINY
      - POL.CH. MATROS Z KORDEGARDY
      - POL.CH. DOMKA Z PSIEGO RAJU
  - PLAZA Z KORDEGARDY
    - INT'L.CH AKIS V. PON-GARTEN
      - POL.CH. GROG SPOD ZAGLA
      - POL.CH. CUMA SPOD ZAGLA
    - POL.CH. USTKA Z KORDEGARDY
      - IN.PL.CH DOMAN Z KORDEGARDY
      - DUMKA Z KORDEGARDY

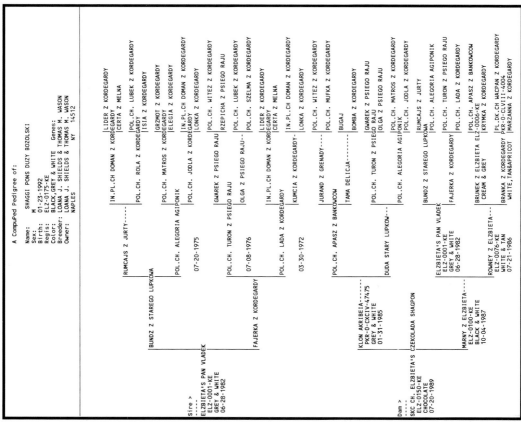

A CompuPed Pedigree of:

Name: SHAGGI PONS DUZY BOZOLSKI
Sex: M
Birth: 01-23-1992
Regis: ELZ-0175-KE
Color: BLACK,GREY & WHITE   Genes:
Breeder: LOANA J. SHIELDS & THOMAS M. WASON
Owner: LOANA J. SHIELDS & THOMAS M. WASON
         NAPLES   NY   14512

Sire >
ELZBIETA'S PAN VLADEK
ELZ-0001-KE
GREY & WHITE
06-28-1982

- BUNDZ Z STAREGO LUPKOWA
  - RUMCAJS Z JURTY
    - IN.PL.CH DOMAN Z KORDEGARDY
      - LIDER Z KORDEGARDY
      - CERTA Z MELNA
    - POL.CH. ROLA Z KORDEGARDY
      - POL.CH. LUBEK Z KORDEGARDY
      - ISIA Z KORDEGARDY
  - POL.CH. ALEGORIA AGIPONIK 07-20-1975
    - POL.CH. MATROS Z KORDEGARDY
      - GRZMOT Z KORDEGARDY
      - ELEGIA Z KORDEGARDY
    - POL.CH. JOOLA Z KORDEGARDY
      - IN.PL.CH DOMAN Z KORDEGARDY
      - LONKA Z KORDEGARDY
- FAJERKA Z KORDEGARDY
  - POL.CH. TURON Z PSIEGO RAJU 07-08-1976
    - GWAREK Z PSIEGO RAJU
      - POL.CH. WITEZ Z KORDEGARDY
      - RZEPICHA Z PSIEGO RAJU
    - OLGA Z PSIEGO RAJU
      - POL.CH. LUBEK Z KORDEGARDY
      - POL.CH. SZELMA Z KORDEGARDY
  - POL.CH. LADA Z KORDEGARDY 03-30-1972
    - IN.PL.CH DOMAN Z KORDEGARDY
      - LIDER Z KORDEGARDY
      - CERTA Z MELNA
    - KUMCIA Z KORDEGARDY
      - POL.CH. LUBEK Z KORDEGARDY
      - DUDA Z KORDEGARDY

Dam >
SKC CH. ELZBIETA SHAGPON
ELZ-0150-KE
CHOCOLATE
07-20-1989

- CZEKOLADA SHAGPON
  - KLON AKRIBEIA
    PKR-0-CXCIV-47475
    GREY & WHITE
    01-31-1985
    - POL.CH. APASZ Z BANKOWCOW
      - JURAND Z GRENADY
      - TAMA DELICJA
    - DUDA STARY LUPKOW
      - POL.CH. TURON Z PSIEGO RAJU
        - GWAREK Z PSIEGO RAJU
        - OLGA Z PSIEGO RAJU
      - POL.CH. ALEGORIA AGIPONIK
        - POL.CH. MATROS Z KORDEGARDY
        - POL.CH. JOOLA Z KORDEGARDY
  - ELZBIETA'S PAN VLADEK
    ELZ-0001-KE
    GREY & WHITE
    06-28-1982
    - BUNDZ Z STAREGO LUPKOW
      - RUMCAJS Z JURTY
      - POL.CH. ALEGORIA AGIPONIK
    - FAJERKA Z KORDEGARDY
      - POL.CH. TURON Z PSIEGO RAJU
      - POL.CH. LADA Z KORDEGARDY
- MARNY Z ELZBIETA
  ELZ-0100-KE
  BLACK & WHITE
  10-04-1987
  - ROWNEY Z ELZBIETA
    ELZ-0076-KE
    WHITE & TAN
    07-21-1986
    - BRUNEK Z ELZBIETA ELZ-0006-KE
      CREAM & GREY
      - POL.CH. APASZ Z BANKOWCOW
      - KRYMKA Z KORDEGARDY
    - BRANKA Z KORDEGARDY
      WHITE,TAN&APRICOT
      - PL.DK.CH WACPAN Z KORDEGARDY
      - MARZANNA Z KORDEGARDY

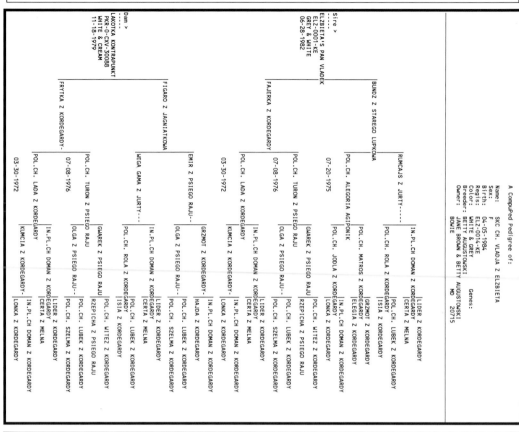

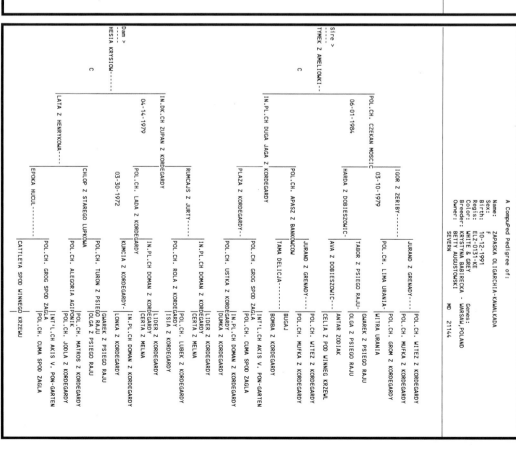

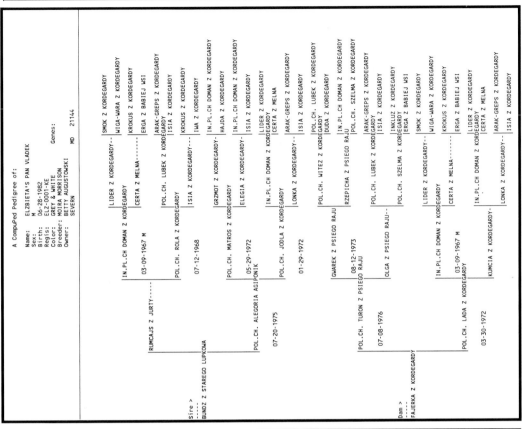

A CompuPed Pedigree of:

Name: ELZBIETA'S PAN VLADEK
Sex: M
Birth: 06-28-1982
Regis: ELZ-0001-KE
Color: GREY & WHITE
Breeder: MOIRA MORRISON
Owner: BETTY AUGUSTOWSKI
                           SEVERN   MD   21144   Genes:

Sire >

BUNDZ Z STAREGO LUPKOWA

RUMCAJS Z JURTY-----

IN.PL.CH DOMAN Z KORDEGARDY
03-09-1967 M
LIDER Z KORDEGARDY-----
  SMOK Z KORDEGARDY
  WIGA-WARA Z KORDEGARDY
CERTA Z MELNA-----
  KROKUS Z KORDEGARDY
  ERGA Z BABIEJ WSI

POL.CH. ROLA Z KORDEGARDY
07-12-1968
POL.CH. LUBEK Z KORDEGARDY
  ARAK-GREPS Z KORDEGARDY
  ISIA Z KORDEGARDY
ISIA Z KORDEGARDY
  KROKUS Z KORDEGARDY
  IWA Z KORDEGARDY

POL.CH. ALEGORIA AGIPONIK

POL.CH. MATROS Z KORDEGARDY
05-29-1972
GRZMOT Z KORDEGARDY-
  IN.PL.CH DOMAN Z KORDEGARDY
  HAJDA Z KORDEGARDY
ELEGIA Z KORDEGARDY-
  IN.PL.CH DOMAN Z KORDEGARDY
  ISIA Z KORDEGARDY

POL.CH. JODLA Z KORDEGARDY
01-29-1972
IN.PL.CH DOMAN Z KORDEGARDY
  LIDER Z KORDEGARDY
  CERTA Z MELNA
LONKA Z KORDEGARDY--
  ARAK-GREPS Z KORDEGARDY
  ISIA Z KORDEGARDY

Dam >

FAJERKA Z KORDEGARDY

POL.CH. TURON Z PSIEGO RAJU

GWAREK Z PSIEGO RAJU
08-12-1973
RZEPICHA Z PSIEGO RAJU
  POL.CH. WITEZ Z KORDEGARDY
  DUDA Z KORDEGARDY
  IN.PL.CH DOMAN Z KORDEGARDY
  POL.CH. SZELMA Z KORDEGARDY

OLGA Z PSIEGO RAJU--
07-08-1976
POL.CH. LUBEK Z KORDEGARDY
  ARAK-GREPS Z KORDEGARDY
  ISIA Z KORDEGARDY
POL.CH. SZELMA Z KORDEGARDY
  INKLUZ Z KORDEGARDY
  ERGA Z BABIEJ WSI

POL.CH. LADA Z KORDEGARDY

IN.PL.CH DOMAN Z KORDEGARDY
03-09-1967 M
LIDER Z KORDEGARDY-----
  SMOK Z KORDEGARDY
  WIGA-WARA Z KORDEGARDY
CERTA Z MELNA-----
  KROKUS Z KORDEGARDY
  ERGA Z BABIEJ WSI

KUMCIA Z KORDEGARDY
03-30-1972
IN.PL.CH DOMAN Z KORDEGARDY
  LIDER Z KORDEGARDY
  CERTA Z MELNA
LONKA Z KORDEGARDY-
  ARAK-GREPS Z KORDEGARDY
  ISIA Z KORDEGARDY

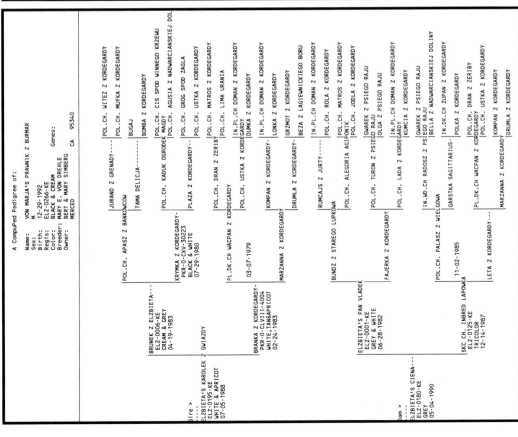

A CompuPed Pedigree of:

Name: VON MARJA'S PRAWNIK Z BURMAR
Sex: M
Birth: 12-29-1992
Regis: ELZ-0266-KE
Color: BLACK & CREAM
Breeder: MARY E. VON DREHLE
Owner: BERT & MARY SIMBERG
                          MERCED   CA   95340   Genes:

Sire >

ELZBIETA'S KAROLEK Z GWIAZDY
ELZ-0195-KE
WHITE & APRICOT
07-05-1988

BRUNEK Z ELZBIETA---
ELZ-0006-KE
CREAM & GREY
04-19-1983

POL.CH. APASZ Z BANKOWCOW

JURAND Z GRENADY-----
  POL.CH. WITEZ Z KORDEGARDY
  POL.CH. MUFKA Z KORDEGARDY
TAMA DELICJA-------
  BUGAJ
  BOMBA Z KORDEGARDY

KRYMKA Z KORDEGARDY-
PKR-0-CKV-30223
BLACK & WHITE
07-29-1980
POL.CH. KADUK OGRODEK MAGDY
  CIS SPOD WINNEGO KRZEWU
  POL.CH. AGUSIA Z NADWARCIANSKIEJ DOL
PLAZA Z KORDEGARDY--
  POL.CH. GROG SPOD ZAGLA
  POL.CH. USTKA Z KORDEGARDY

BRANKA Z KORDEGARDY-
PKR-0-CLVIII-4004
WHITE,TAN&APRICOT
02-24-1983

PL.DK.CH WACPAN Z KORDEGARDY
03-07-1979
POL.CH. DRAN Z ZERIBY
  POL.CH. MATROS Z KORDEGARDY
  POL.CH. LIMA URANIA
POL.CH. USTKA Z KORDEGARDY
  IN.PL.CH DOMAN Z KORDEGARDY
  DUMKA Z KORDEGARDY

MARZANNA Z KORDEGARDY
KOMPAN Z KORDEGARDY-
  IN.PL.CH DOMAN Z KORDEGARDY
  LONKA Z KORDEGARDY
DRUMLA Z KORDEGARDY-
  GRZMOT Z KORDEGARDY
  BEZA Z LAGIEWNICKIEGO BORU

Dam >

ELZBIETA'S CIENA---
ELZ-0180-KE
GREY
05-04-1990

ELZBIETA'S PAN VLADEK
ELZ-0001-KE
GREY & WHITE
06-28-1982

BUNDZ Z STAREGO LUPKOWA

RUMCAJS Z JURTY-----
  POL.CH. ROLA Z KORDEGARDY
  POL.CH. WITEZ Z KORDEGARDY
POL.CH. ALEGORIA AGIPONIK
  POL.CH. MATROS Z KORDEGARDY
  POL.CH. JODLA Z KORDEGARDY

FAJERKA Z KORDEGARDY
POL.CH. TURON Z PSIEGO RAJU
  GWAREK Z PSIEGO RAJU
  OLGA Z PSIEGO RAJU
POL.CH. LADA Z KORDEGARDY
  IN.PL.CH DOMAN Z KORDEGARDY
  KUMCIA Z KORDEGARDY

SKC.CH. INBRED LAPONKA
ELZ-0125-KE
TRICOLOR
12-14-1987

POL.CH. PALASZ Z WIELGOWA
11-02-1985
IN.WD.CH RADOSZ Z PSIEGO RAJU
  GWAREK Z PSIEGO RAJU
  BELLA Z NADWARCIANSKIEJ DOLINY
GARSTKA SAGITTARIUS-
  IN.DK.CH ZUPAN Z KORDEGARDY
  POLKA Z KORDEGARDY

LETA Z KORDEGARDY---
PL.DK.CH WACPAN Z KORDEGARDY
  POL.CH. DRAN Z ZERIBY
  POL.CH. USTKA Z KORDEGARDY
MARZANNA Z KORDEGARDY
  KOMPAN Z KORDEGARDY
  DRUMLA Z KORDEGARDY

Index

Page numbers in **boldface** refer to illustrations.

H-1091, 912 pp
over 1100 color photos

TS-175, 896 pp
over 1300 color photos

TS-204, 160 pp
over 50 line drawings

TS-205, 156 pp
over 130 color photos

H-1106, 544pp
over 400 color photos

TS-212, 256 pp
over 140 color photos

TS-220, 64 pp
over 50 color illus.

PS-872, 240 pp
178 color illus.

H-1095, 272 pp
over 160 color illus.

KW-227, 96 pp
100 color photos

H-1016, 224 pp
135 photos

TW-113, 256 pp
200 color photos

H-962, 255 pp
nearly 100 photos

PS-607, 254 pp
136 B & W photos

TS-101, 192 pp
over 100 photos

TW-102, 256 pp
over 200 color photos

SK-044, 64 pp
over 50 color
photos

TS-130, 160 pp
50 color illus.

H-1061, 608 pp
100 B & W photos

H-969, 224 pp
62 color photos